Seven Vi...

YES

*Difficult Decisions,
Mediations and Negotiations
Made Easier*

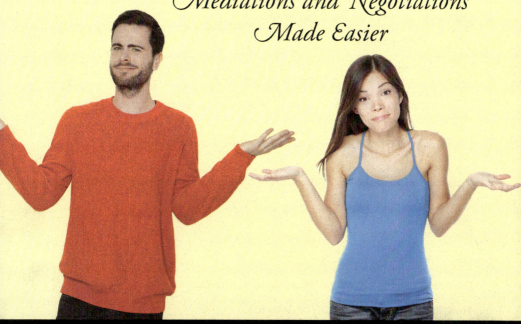

JANET MILLER WISEMAN LICSW,
Certified Family and Divorce Mediator

The opinions expressed in this manuscript are solely the opinions of the author and do not represent the opinions or thoughts of the publisher. The author has represented and warranted full ownership and/or legal right to publish all the materials in this book.

Seven Visual Steps to Yes
Difficult Decisions, Mediations and Negotiations Made Easier
All Rights Reserved.
Copyright © 2016 Janet Miller Wiseman LICSW, Certified Family and Divorce Mediator
v7.0

Cover Photo © 2016 thinkstockphotos.com. All rights reserved - used with permission.

This book may not be reproduced, transmitted, or stored in whole or in part by any means, including graphic, electronic, or mechanical without the express written consent of the publisher except in the case of brief quotations embodied in critical articles and reviews.

Outskirts Press, Inc.
http://www.outskirtspress.com

ISBN: 978-1-4787-7173-9

Outskirts Press and the "OP" logo are trademarks belonging to Outskirts Press, Inc.

PRINTED IN THE UNITED STATES OF AMERICA

DEDICATIONS

*John Adams Fiske, Attorney,
for you to know what I do after you refer couples to me.
To Kathryn A. George and Marilyn Booth-King,
special friends and colleagues who help me with my work and life.
To Todd, Melissa, Andrew, and Tucker Wiseman,
my precious family.*

Table of Contents

Prologue i

Chapter 1:   Did You Say You Have a Conflict? 1

Chapter 2:   Adnan and Sherrie Expand the Pie
from Negotiation of an In-Law Apartment 2

Chapter 3:   Laura and Caleb's Vacation Dilemma:
The Mountains or the Shore 9

Chapter 4:   What the Heck Are "Supposals" and "Proposals"? 19

Chapter 5:   Sophie and Seth Work toward
a Creative Separation 22

Chapter 6:   Anne and Sam "We Are Going to Kill One
Another If We Don't Separate Immediately" 29

Chapter 7:   The Importance of Step II:
Bottom-Line Basic Human Needs 35

Chapter 8:   "Compromise" Does Not Belong in
the Seven Visual Steps to Yes 42

Chapter 9:   "I'm Pregnant ... and ..." 44

Chapter 10:   "She's Not Pregnant ... but ..." 51

Chapter 11:   Bill and Sally's Divorce: Sally Wants Not to
Be a Bag Lady; Bill Wants a Fair Share 57

Chapter 12:   Mediation versus Negotiation 71

Chapter 13:   Negotiating the Impossible Vacation Agenda 75

Chapter 14:   Baseball or Violin for Marco? 82

Chapter 15:   The Seven Visual Steps: Skeleton and Muscle 88

Chapter 16:   Can We Afford a Garage and a Vacation? 93

Chapter 17:   The Importance of Being Earnest
              When Using the 1—5 Rating Systems 99
Chapter 18:   Origins of the Seven Visual Steps to Yes 100
Afterword..107
Acknowledgments 109
Index I 111
Index II 112
Bibliography...114

Prologue

I'm going to tell you a story. It was April 15, 2013, the day of the bombing at the Boston Marathon finish line. There was a stunned, upsetting, eerie feeling in the air that continued on April 16 when the police were searching for the alleged bomber. Bostonians and those of us in the suburbs were "locked down", told to stay inside our homes while the search was on. Eventually, a man in Watertown, Massachusetts, who had stepped out onto his front porch, noticed the plastic covering on his boat had been disturbed. Dzhokhar Tsarnaev, a Chechnyan immigrant, was discovered inside the boat with an alleged inscription on a bloody note: "The US government is killing our innocent civilians…I can't stand to see such evil go unpunished. We Muslims are one body, you hurt one of us, you hurt us all…"

April 15 is the anniversary of the "shot heard round the world" in Lexington, Massachusetts, 241 years ago in 1775 when the Massachusetts Bay Colony earned its independence from Great Britain on the Lexington Green, near where I live. The convergence of dates when guns and bombs were detonated seemed a strange, yet apt coincidence.

Two brothers from Chechnya had detonated the bombs that day, killing three people and causing many, many injuries, amputations, and blindness. We knew that the Pilgrims from England and the family from Chechnya both were seeking to make their own way in the world, valuing the opportunities that coming to a new land might offer, including relief from religious oppression. The Puritan Pilgrims felt oppressed by the Church of England, and we know that Chechnyan Muslims in Russia were scorned. Here the parallels between the two groups may end.

We knew the Pilgrims were seeking religious freedom and independence as a colony. The Tsarnaevs' father wanted the opportunity for his eldest son, who died on April 16, to be a distinguished, perhaps even an Olympic athlete, and his youngest son to be an "Ivy League scholar."

The Harvard University Program on Negotiation conference, "Confronting Evil," scheduled for April 16 and 17, was postponed until April 17, 2013, two days after the bombing and shortened by a day.

At the cocktail hour, after the panel discussion on "Confronting Evil," I told a colleague that I was writing this book to share the seven visual steps for highly effective negotiation and decision-making with "the man on the street," us ordinary folks. He responded, "You don't want to do that; the book will get stuck on the self-improvement shelves." I replied, "Exactly! For over thirty years my clients have been benefiting from these visual principles, reaching resolutions for all kinds of differences, disputes, and conflicts, and making important decisions. I want to make the approach widely available to everyone, not just to academics, business executives, international negotiators, diplomats, and people like us, who frequent academic conferences like this conference today!"

I shared with my colleague how amazing it has been to witness partners, indeed disputants of all kinds, making decisions, resolving conflicts, and solving problems using the initial (1) Getting to Yes, (2) Mutual Gains, and (3) *The Art and Science of Negotiation* approaches. I redesigned, amplified, and put into more user-friendly language those approaches and made them into a visual format. I told my colleague that after standing on the shoulders of the giants in the negotiation field—one of whom was participating in the "Confronting Evil" conference that day—I had synthesized the negotiation process into seven easy-to-comprehend steps. I had made them visual, made the names of steps more colloquial, and had been teaching the principles directly and indirectly in my office to clients of family, divorce, decision-making, and business mediation, as well as psychotherapy and counseling clients.

Of course, I also use the Seven Visual Steps to Yes to make my own decisions and resolve personal conflicts. Many of my clients have given me permission to share their stories. Their identities are disguised. All conflicts, problems, and decisions described here share one outcome: they have been successful. The partners have improved their relationships or made decisions to restructure their families, businesses, and lives, all using the same seven-step visual model for highly effective negotiation, conflict resolution, and decision-making. Most of the partners who have used this seven-step model in mediation and negotiation, in fact, have creatively resolved their conflicts and made decisions.

While at the cocktail hour I also met a quiet-spoken, well-dressed man. Bob Mnookin, a Harvard Law School professor, whisked by and said, "Janet, you don't want to miss this man's talk on Ecuador at the JFK Center for International Studies!" Certainly not, I thought. I think of Ecuador as a second home, having taught mediation and negotiation at a law school and a family institute in Quito, and having lived with Quechan Indians in the rain forest near Tena, Ecuador, on two separate occasions. I asked the well-dressed gentleman, "What do you do here?" He replied, "Well, I teach at the Harvard Law School and the JFK Center." I proceeded to ask, "And what did you do in Ecuador?" Again, he answered, "Well, I was in politics." I felt the need to ask him and so I said, "And what role did you play?" "Well," he answered, "I was president." I wasn't quite expecting that! Then he added, "And I was mayor of Quito, the capital, for eight years."

I shared with President Mahuad some of my astonishing experiences while living in the jungle of Ecuador, including a fire believed to be an arson with two little girls killed and a shaman who came to live with me for six months who had had surgery for a hepatoma in 1998 and who was still alive. After our talk I went back to the office to do an Internet search. I discovered that eleven weeks after his election as president of Ecuador, Jamil Mahuad had negotiated the final boundary between Ecuador and Peru with Alberto Fujimori, president of Peru; Bill Clinton, US president; and Roger Fisher, a Harvard Law School professor. These four men assisted with the negotiations of the frontier beween the two countries, which had been in dispute since 1821, for 177 years. The boundary was set in stone on October 26, 1998.

After the frontier was settled, the indigenous tribal people who had lost their lands in the negotiation, along with military personnel, descended upon Quito to protest the new frontier and their loss of land. Allegedly President Mahuad left or "fled" to the more comfortable confines of academia at Harvard University. On a macro level, using the same techniques I use in my office, Mahuad had settled an important international frontier dispute that had been brewing for several centuries. He and President Fujimori received a Nobel Prize for their work in resolution of the conflict.

Each and every day in my office, I facilitate the settlement of disputes that are just as important to the participants, on a micro level, as the settling of an international frontier—and probably even more so to the participants. This book is full of diverse conflicts that you already have encountered or may encounter in your life. If you follow the seven steps, you will find yourself becoming a successful negotiator and a dynamite decision-maker.

CHAPTER 1
Did You Say You Have a Conflict?

The Seven Visual Steps to Yes

Who doesn't have conflicts? Everyone has issues, conflicts, problems, and decisions to make, from minor ones like where to go on your next vacation to more major ones involving, say, marriage. For instance, a fiancée desperately wants to get married, but her fiancé fears a third divorce; indeed, the fiancé fears "a heart attack at the altar" if they don't get some important issues resolved. Of the hundreds of real-life conflicts presenting in my office, some of the issues have been: Where shall we take our vacation this year? Do we add onto our home in which her mother can live, buy a house or condo for her several streets away, or help her locate a pleasant senior residential home? Can I hire help to finish the new house in order to spend more time with her, or must I do it all myself as a form of relaxation and to save money? "We Greeks always prefer to save money, honey. You know that!"

Many people have issues and conflicts during a separation or divorce, such as when and with whom the children shall live during a marital separation or after the divorce, and how to fairly divide a great deal or small amount of marital assets. How to create a collective vision of what a time-limited marital separation will look like is a decision-making situation ideal for the Seven Visual Steps model. Who gets to stay in the marital home? The husband who designed it but does not have enough income for expenses until he receives his inheritance, or the wife who isn't especially attached to the home but could afford to buy out her husband's interest? How does a couple come to understand that they will have enough financial resources to survive until the end of their lives?

In each of these examples, with names and identifying features changed, I used the Seven Visual Steps to Yes approach with the parties involved in the conflict, and each one reached a creative and interesting outcome.

CHAPTER 2

Adnan and Sherrie Expand the Pie from Negotiation of an In-Law Apartment

In this chapter I will describe the Seven Visual Steps to Yes model, using the example of whether or not Adnan and Sherrie should build an addition to their home for her mother. In the subsequent chapters I will share with you many other cases where the seven-step process was used—some cases in which the process was fairly hilarious!

Before you start to use the seven-step model, *always define* the conflict, issue, problem, or decision you are trying to resolve: "the conflict, issue, problem, or decision is…" This comes before Step I, and is the overarching *definition* of the conflict, problem, issue, or decision.

Only after defining the decision to be made, the conflict, issue, or problem to be resolved are you ready to move through the Seven Visual Steps to Yes model illustrated below.

Adnan and Sherrie, a couple in their mid-forties, without children, came into the office specifically for decision-making mediation. Sherrie's seventy-five-year-old mother, Edith, was healthy, engaging, and self-sufficient, and she wanted to live near some part of her family. Her other two adult children lived outside the country. She had attempted to get a visa to live near one of her three children, one in Luxembourg, the other in Indonesia, but those options turned out to be out of the question. She hadn't out and out asked Adnan and Sherrie if she should or could come to live with or near them, but they both were feeling some pressure to talk about this possibility in case Sherrie's mom did bring up the subject with them.

Adnan, whose culture promoted three generations or more living together, saw this as a wonderful opportunity to build an in-law apartment onto the house and include Sherrie's mother in the family, as well as add a painting studio for Sherrie and a woodworking shop for him. However, when they came to the office, they were not happy.

Sherrie's Step I goal, what she *wanted*, was to investigate the living arrangement options in their community for her mother. Adnan's Step I goal, what he *wanted*, was to build an in-law addition to their home with a painting studio and a woodworking shop. He was clearly excited.

Step I: "I Want" Positions

She wants:	**He wants:**
Sherrie	**Adnan**

- To explore the options in our community where my mother might want to live.
- "To travel."

- "Build an in-law addition with a woodworking shop for me and a painting studio for Sherrie so we can have spaces to express our creativity."

Step II: My Bottom-Line Need

When asked what she *needed* (Step II), Sherrie forcefully stated that their mortgage was paid off, and she *needed* not to incur more housing debt at this stage of her life. Adnan said, "Travel is for old people! I'm a homebody and so are you. We *need* spaces to express our creativity most of the year while we're at home. We aren't going to be traveling that much until retirement!" Sherrie looked dumbfounded. Her husband was not going to go along passively with her this time; she could see that. Adnan said he needed space to express himself creatively, and he was sure that Sherrie did as well.

What *really, really mattered* (Step III) to Sherrie was that "I preserve my excellent relationship with my mother. I'm afraid if we're all living under the same roof, we will take each other for granted and be in each other's space too much, and I'll lose my close connection with you, Adnan." Adnan was a sociable person with the gift of gab. Sherrie was afraid he would "chat up" her mother too often and leave her out of the conversation.

Step III: What *Really, Really* Matters to Me

"What *really, really* matters to me (Step III) at midlife," Adnan implored, "is that Sherrie and I have our own studios to express our creativity. I might even be able to quit my job and go into cabinetry, as well as having an in-law addition for Sherrie's mom, which will be fun for us and make the house more valuable to sell."

Sherries' eyes rolled to the top of their socketts. "Adnan, we were talking here about whether we build an addition for my mother, and now you're talking painting studio and shop space. You're adding in apples with avocados! I am getting frustrated with you!"

What *really, really* mattered to Sherrie was:
- To preserve her excellent relationship with her mother
- To not interrupt her close connection with Adnan

Step IV: Best Personal Alternative

Adnan spoke first. If he couldn't negotiate adding on space for her mother, a studio for Sherrie, and a woodworking shop for himself, he would build a top-notch woodworking shop in the basement, upgrading the primitive one already there, using the inheritance money Uncle Ted left him. He didn't need to add on another mortgage.

Sherrie kept her Step IV best personal alternative to herself, letting us know later that it would be to research both condominiums and apartments near their home and post-fifty-five retirement homes. Her mother was way too young physically and at heart for assisted living facilities, and Sherrie couldn't see them taking on more mortgage responsibility.

Sherrie and Adnan were ready to begin Step V, their brainstorming of creative options.

Step V: Brainstorming

	BRAINSTORMING CREATIVE OPTIONS and IDEAS	Sherrie	Adnan
1.	Sherrie: "I know for sure that I don't want to incur more housing debt just when our mortgage is paid off."	5	1
2.	Adnan: "I would love to have your mother living in an addition with us."	2	5
3.	Sherrie: "You seem so gung-ho about having a workshop here. We're talking about an in-law addition."	1	5
4.	Sherrie: "If a shop is such a big deal, why not use the money your Uncle Ted gave you and build the shop in the basement?"	2	5
5.	Adnan: "I'd like to have lots of light and air in my shop!"	1	5
6.	Sherrie: "It's more important to have light and air in a painting studio, but that's *not* what we're talking about here!"	2	5

Sherrie and Adnan had "gone outside the connecting dots" and expanded the idea of building an addition for her mother to investigating a new post-fifty-five retirement community several miles from their home, as well as apartments and condominiums nearer their home. After all, they had no real idea whether or not her mother would prefer living with others or having her own space, or even if she would desire to live near them or with them. If and when the subject of Sherrie's mother moving closer to them came up, they would be prepared with some options and pictures of those options. They circled options two, four, and six on their brainstorming list; although not very close to one another, they were the only options that were even somewhat close to one another.

Step VI: Agreement Building—Supposals and Proposals

The pair moved rapidly to Step VI. Adnan supposed that he would build his workshop in the basement, and a sauna as well, with funds he had inherited from his uncle Ted. In addition, he proposed putting skylights in their upstairs bedroom and the library and converting the library to a painting studio for Sherrie in the next several years—for her light and air. In exchange, he and Sherrie would get hot, relaxing, steamed air in the sauna when the funds were available. He would take charge of investigating the post-fifty-five retirement community, which he had heard was outfitted with a stage, a movie theater, and a deep, long swimming pool, and had a requirement that residents take at least one college or graduate course a semester. Sherrie had to admit that this sounded like a place that Edith, her mother, would take to. Sherrie gasped at how creative Adnan was becoming.

Sherrie proposed that she would look at apartments and condos that were nearer to their home than the retirement community. She wanted to have some options for her mother in case Edith didn't want to be around a lot of people.

They agreed that Adnan would look at Ledgewood Acres, the retirement community, and Sherrie would look at the apartments and condominiums. They would have pictures and could be specific if and when the subject of Edith moving nearby arose. In addition, Sherrie favored Adnan building his shop and sauna, as well as putting in skylights in their bedroom and converting the library to her studio in two or three years—all using Uncle Ted's bequest to Adnan and not incurring any indebtedness. What had begun as a question of building an in-law apartment had turned into remodeling their home for their mutual creativity, with Adnan's inheritance and without taking on any new mortgage debt. They also had plans to explore other options where Sherrie's mother might want to live.

Sherrie and Adnan had "gone outside the connecting dots," expanding on the idea of having her mother live with them by building an addition onto their home, to investigating both a new post-fifty-five retirement community several miles from their home and some apartments and condominiums nearer their home. If and when the subject of her moving closer to them came up, they would be prepared with some options and pictures of those options. They circled numbers two, four, and six on the brainstorming list, as they were the only options even close to mutual agreement, although they weren't rated as fives or fours or even a three and a five.

Step VII: A Mutual Agreement

> Adnan will look into post-fifty-five retirement communities and Sherrie will look into condominiums and apartments near their home for Sherrie's mother. Adnan will build a woodworking shop with money from Uncle Ted, and they will think about a painting studio for Sherrie over the next few years.
>
> *Peace Begins with Us*

I have been employing the Seven Visual Steps to Yes in family and divorce mediation, couples mediation, couples psychotherapy, and individual psychotherapy for over thirty-five years. I use it in my own life too. I am sharing with you real-life conflicts and decisions that have been made using this model so that you, too, can clearly see that it works, gain solid belief in it, and begin to incorporate it into your lives for big and small conflicts and to make decisions. The more cases you can visualize, the easier it will be for you to call up the Seven Visual Steps to Yes approach when you are making a decision or resolving a conflict, problem, or an issue.

The smallest conflict I've ever mediated in my office had caused newlyweds to disinvite relatives on both sides of their families for

Christmas dinner. This really happened. They were in conflict about where to erect their first Christmas tree after their marriage. Imagine, a really serious, angry conflict about where to locate a Christmas tree! I could scarcely believe it! Using the model, they resolved the conflict, erected the tree in just the right place for both of them, and reissued the invitations for Christmas dinner.

Examples of larger conflicts involved whether a couple should stay together after a marital affair. One member of the couple wanted to stay together; the other decided on a marital separation to gain perspective, and eventually the couple happily reconciled. One couple used the Seven Visual Steps to Yes model to decide to divorce and, believe it or not, returned five years later to use the model again and decided to remarry. I know it happened because they invited me to the wedding reception, which I attended. Yet another couple, whose divorce I mediated, came back later; although they planned to remain divorced and live in two separate houses, they wanted to write a contract regarding how to maintain an exclusive and primary relationship while divorced. Still another couple wrote, signed, and executed their divorce agreement, and maintained separate residences and a summer home together, but never divorced. Instead they rewrote rules for their separated lives together.

CHAPTER 3
Laura and Caleb's Vacation Dilemma: The Mountains or the Shore

Laura and Caleb were a bright and thoughtful couple in their late thirties and early forties. They had established themselves in their careers, she as a radiologist and he as an environmental science field engineer. They had two children: Abe, age four, and Hannah, age seven.

The early spring in which they came to my office, Laura and Caleb were trying to decide whether to attempt to have a third child. During our process, they were each offered vacation time at the same time for the last two weeks of July. They were eager to plan a vacation that would meet the needs of the whole family. Before being asked, Laura announced that she *wanted* (Step I) a family vacation hiking Mount Katahdin in Maine, where her father had always taken her and her younger sister, Margret, as teenagers. Her father had died the past summer, and she was awaiting an opportunity to spread his ashes on one of their favorite peaks, her Step II, bottom-line need.

Caleb *wanted* (Step I) a family vacation as well, but he *wanted* to go to their traditional Martha's Vineyard cottage in West Tisbury *to rest* from his taxing travel schedule, his Step II, bottom-line, basic human need. He was already savoring seafood on the grill and the prospect of reading, then dozing off with his book on his nose, while the children played in the gentle waves. He said he could smell the Vineyard already.

Caleb had no trouble answering that his bottom-line need, Step II, was also rest. He said he was utterly exhausted and burned out from the traveling and fieldwork required of his job. Laura was more than clear in stating that her job was sedentary, in a dark enclosed basement of the hospital, and that she needed to actively move outdoors. She *wanted* to hike Mount Katahdin, her Step I, and her Step II bottom-line needs were to scatter her father's ashes and to begin moving and lose some weight before giving a presentation in the fall.

Caleb interjected that recently he had been walking up the back steps to the family room when he heard moaning and groaning coming through the screen door. He saw Laura lying collapsed on the floor. Had she had a heart attack or an accident? "No," she growled, "these crunches and leg lifts just aren't going to work. I *need* to get back to hiking, the only thing that really helps me to take off weight from not moving, from being sedentary."

Although the first two steps of the Seven Visual Steps to Yes may seem like the same question, they aren't. Wanting and needing are two different things. Needing is more basic, more fundamental. When both questions are asked, people just know the difference and are quick to respond. No one has ever commented that the two questions are the same.

When asked what *really, really* mattered to each of them (Step III), Laura answered first. What mattered to her was to get in shape for a presentation she was making at a medical conference in the fall. She had gained "baby belly weight" during her two pregnancies. She wanted desperately to lose the weight and was determined that hiking this summer would be her fitness starting point. It also mattered to scatter her father's ashes on Mount Katahdin where he had hiked so many summers with her and her sister. This would be deeply meaningful to her.

Without waiting to be asked, Caleb interjected that what *really, really* mattered to him was the opportunity to rest, to stay put, to catch up on his casual reading, and to be with Laura, Abe, and Hannah on the beach in their traditional cottage, with the children playing contently in the sand, running in and out of the waves. He added that he loved to prepare shrimp kebabs, beer-infused chicken, grass-fed beef, and vegetables on the grill and go out to the same local restaurants for seafood where they and their friends had eaten for years. Caleb's basic human need and what really mattered to him were the same: to rest in West Tisbury, Martha's Vineyard. He would frequently quote the Spanish proverb "How beautiful it is to do nothing and then rest afterward."

It was obvious that Laura and Caleb's needs and desires for a family vacation were very different. They were caught between deep needs for rest, on the one hand, and for activity on the other hand. Would they be able to negotiate a mutual agreement in which these seemingly polarized needs could be met? They were stuck, they knew it, and both of them were very unhappy, sometimes believing that the other person was the problem instead of their own deeply felt and polarized needs.

When asked their "best personal alternative" (Step IV), what they could do if they couldn't make a deal for a vacation with their spouse, Caleb indicated that it would be to take four-year-old Abe to North Carolina, where his parents had a home on a lake, and to ask Caleb's younger sister, Halle, also with a home on the lake, to help him and his parents with child care for the whole two-week vacation. Laura could come down for the second week with Hannah after they had hiked up Mount Katahdin and spread her father's ashes. If she wanted to continue to hike in North Carolina, do activities such as Zumba or Pilates, jog, and participate in a family vacation, she could continue her fitness/weight loss program. Laura's personal best alternative was surprisingly similar when we learned of it later. She would have enlisted her sister, Margret, who loved to hike Mount Katahdin and loved Hannah and Abe, to hike with them for one or the whole two weeks, helping out with the children. She and Margret could scatter their father's ashes, and Caleb could do whatever the heck he wanted to do! She was angry that Caleb wasn't being more accommodating to her needs. In her heart of hearts, she knew she could hike for a week with Margret and then go to North Carolina to be with Caleb, the children, and his family, but she wasn't letting on that this would be a possibility.

Caleb heaved a sigh a relief when he thought of his personal best alternative, getting the rest he needed, even if he had to take all or part of his vacation separately. He needed rest desperately. Laura giggled when she contemplated getting what she wanted, getting in shape, no matter what. She needed to look svelte and professional for her medical presentation.

Step V: Brainstorming
We were now at Step V, generating creative options and ideas whether sane or silly.

	BRAINSTORMING CREATIVE OPTIONS and IDEAS	Laura:	Caleb:
1.	Laura: "Two weeks hiking with the whole family at Mount Katahdin."	5	1
2.	Caleb: "Two delicious weeks relaxing at Martha's Vineyard."	1	5
3.	Laura: "Whole family to Mount Katahdin, Caleb can hike as much or as little as he wants. My sister, Margret, will be invited to hike and to help with the children."	5	2
4.	Caleb: "I go to Martha's Vineyard for two delicious weeks. Laura flies in for the second week to jog and relax 'if she can'."	2	5
5.	Laura: "The whole family needs to be together for two weeks."	5	4-5
6.	Caleb: "I'll rest on Martha's Vineyard for 2 weeks. Laura will fly in with the children the second week; she can jog, do yoga, Zumba, Pilates, whatever."	3	3
7.	Caleb: "I go to North Carolina for two weeks, taking one or both children. My parents and sister, Halle, will *love* to spend time with and care for the children. Laura can come to North Carolina and climb mountains and be active the second week."	4-5	4-5
8.	Caleb: "This is getting WAY too complicated. Let Janet decide." ☺	5	5
9.	Caleb offered to stay at Martha's Vineyard with Abe the whole two weeks. Hannah could go with Laura the first week, and the two of them could come for the traditional Vineyard beach vacation the second week.	4	5
10.	Laura offered that both children go to the beach with Caleb for two weeks.	3	1
11.	Caleb: "Maybe you're not hearing me, Laura. I can barely take care of myself, let alone two children!"	1	1

When it was time to evaluate their rated options, we circled those that were close enough together, and closest to fives, to keep as mutual options. They were numbers five, seven, and nine. The first four options were eliminated. Caleb's having the opportunity to rest had two fives circled.

Laura was ready to make a "supposal" as Step VI, Building the Agreement. She said she could hear and finally *truly* empathize with how exhausted Caleb really was. Caleb interjected that he needed to sleep on the beach with a beer for the whole two weeks. Laura continued by saying she understood that his bottom-line basic *need* for rest was more important to him even than having the whole family together for the entire time. And her bottom-line basic *need* to move, to be active, to hike Mount Katahdin, and to scatter her father's ashes, potentially losing weight in the process, was even more important to her than being together for the whole two weeks of vacation. What a surprise! This was something very difficult for Laura to see and admit, that getting their individual needs met just might have a higher priority than spending the whole two weeks together. Both Caleb and Laura had *wanted* the two weeks of family vacation together. Wasn't vacationing together what all families do? Wouldn't people talk if they took parts of their vacation separately? People might think their marriage was in trouble.

After long contemplation, Laura turned to Caleb and said, "Suppose we go to the Eco-Lodge, with the kids going to the Eco-Lodge Camp and you resting the whole time?" Caleb counter-supposed that she and the kids could do that for a week and join him at the beach at Martha's Vineyard where he would chill out for two weeks --option one. This was his favorite option. Laura pressed for a two-week vacation together, saying how important this would be for the family.

Caleb then entered the second stage, the proposal stage, of Step VI: Agreement Building, giving Laura an offer or proposal, which is stronger than a supposal: "Okay, Laura, if I go to the Eco-Lodge, there will be some creative environmental ideas I can get for my work. But I'll only go if I can have the option of taking two and a half or three days tenting by myself at Lily Bay State Park, building myself a man cave, and cooking beef and chicken outside." Laura counter-proposed, "Okay, Caleb, you're on, and just for that, I agree to promise that we will go to our cottage on Martha's Vineyard next year. You call them to reserve the cottage at West Tisbury as soon as you can!" She sighed, weary from the negotiations. Caleb negotiated with Laura that *she* call the owners of the West Tisbury cottage that afternoon to reserve the cottage for the following summer. He was simply too tired to even pick up the phone.

It had been a long and somewhat painful process, but the Worners had arrived at the final step in the Seven Visual Steps to Yes process, a mutual agreement. They were fairly exhausted, but Laura took out her iPhone and called the Eco-Lodge to make reservations for the summer and then called the owners of the Martha's Vineyard cottage to make their reservations for the next summer.

Below is the seven-step process as we detailed it on the white board.

Definition of the Conflict
"Where shall we take our two-week summer vacation this year?"
"The mountains or the shore?"

Step I: "I Want" Positions

She wants: **He wants:**
Laura Caleb

- "I want to go hiking at Mount Katahdin, Maine."
- "I want to go to our traditional cottage at West Tisbury, Martha's Vineyard."

Step II: My Bottom-Line Need

- Laura's bottom-line basic need: to move, be active, to lose weight, and to scatter her father's ashes.
- Caleb's bottom-line basic need: to rest.

Step III: What *Really, Really* Matters to Me
After it is clear what each person's bottom-line *needs* are in the negotiation, they move on to what matters most.

WIFE:	RATE:	HUSBAND:	RATE:
To scatter my father's ashes	5	To rest	5
To lose weight for my autumn presentation	5	To be with my family for the whole two-week vacation	5
To be with my whole family for the two-week vacation	5	To cook shrimp, beer-infused chicken, and grass-fed beef on the grill on the beach	4
To be active, to move, and to be outdoors	5	To be at Martha's Vineyard, West Tisbury	5

Step IV: Best Personal Alternative
For getting the vacation I want and need if I can't negotiate something with my partner.

Laura: Asking my sister, Margret, to hike with me at Katahdin for one or two weeks, helping with the care of the children.

Caleb: Going to my parents' cottage in North Carolina the whole two weeks and having my parents and sister help with the care of Abe or both children. Laura can come down the second week after she has done what she needs to do at Mount Katahdin.

Step V: Brainstorming

This is how I explained step five to Laura and Caleb: "Together, you both suggest sane and silly ideas for resolving the conflict, problem, or issue, or for making the decision. It is *critical* for each of you to evaluate and rate each option from one to five and to indicate how desirable that option is to you. *Do not leave out this rating step.* The rating step may be the most important, the key element of the Seven Visual Steps to Yes.

The options all could get ones or all fives; this isn't a rating *between* options. You then circle the options that get the highest ratings and those ratings that are close to one another as I will indicate in the examples below. The other ideas may be eliminated if they are rated low. If it is a highly rated number for an idea, that will also be indicated.

	BRAINSTORMING CREATIVE OPTIONS and IDEAS	Laura:	Caleb:
1.	Laura: "Two weeks hiking with the whole family at Mt. Katahdin."	5	1
2.	Caleb: "Two delicious weeks beaching/relaxing at Martha's Vineyard".	1	5
3.	Laura: "The whole family will go to Mt. Katahdin. Caleb can hike as much or as little as he wants. My sister, Margret, will be invited to hike and help with the children."	5	2
4.	Caleb: "I go to Martha's Vineyard for two delicious weeks. Laura flies in second week to jog and relax '*if she can*'."	2	5
5.	Laura: "The whole family needs to be together for the whole two weeks."	5	4.5
6.	Caleb: "I'll rest in Martha's Vineyard for two weeks. Laura will fly in with the children, the second week; she can jog, do yoga, Zumba, Pilates, whatever."	3	3
7.	Caleb: "I go to North Carolina for two weeks, taking one or both children. My parents and sister, Halle, will *love* to spend time with and care for the children. Laura can come to North Carolina the second week, jog, hike mountains, do Zumba, whatever. "	4.5	4.5
8.	Caleb: "This is getting too complicated. Let Janet decide." ☺	5	5
9.	Caleb: "I go to the Vineyard for week one, and Laura flies in the second week with Hannah to jog, do yoga, Zumba, whatever."	3	5

Step VI: Agreement Building—Supposals and Proposals

I. SUPPOSALS
   A. Laura said, "Suppose we go to Mount Katahdin lodge and the kids go to Eco-Lodge Camp?"
   B. Caleb counter-supposed that Laura do the above, he'd go to the beach on Martha's Vineyard for two weeks, and she and the kids could join him the second week.

II. PROPOSALS
   A. Suddenly and surprisingly, Caleb proposed that he could get something out of being at the lodge for his environmental work; he could learn some new concepts. So he would go there if the kids were definitely at camp during the day and would promise not to tax him after 4:30 p.m. when they got out of camp. He would build his man cave of a tent at Lily Bay State Park for two and a half or three days.
   B. Laura counter-proposed that this would be more than fine with her, as long as they would take their whole two-week vacation at the traditional beach cottage at Martha's Vineyard the next year.

Step VII: A Mutual Agreement

We're going to Mt. Katahdin July 15–30, where Laura and her sister, Margret, will hike while Hannah and Abe attend the Eco-Green Camp. Caleb will relax, and go to a man-cave-tent for two to three days, if he so desires. Margret will probably stay only one week. We've made reservations for our traditional cottage on Martha's Vineyard for next year.

Peace Begins with Us

I chose Laura and Caleb's conflict in order to illustrate one in which the participants were not hostile toward one another but were a happily married couple, who had radically different needs at this point in time. They really wanted a mutual solution. It was a conflict where they generated a lot of creative options, any of which could have worked for each of them as individuals, but not for all of them as a family. They were happy with the solution and later reported that they had never had a more satisfying vacation in terms of meeting all of their needs. It wasn't the traditional vacation in that it violated what most people think of as a family vacation, being together the whole time, but it worked for the Worners. It met all of their needs.

CHAPTER 4
What the Heck Are "Supposals" and "Proposals"?

In the process of Seven Visual Steps to Yes, we don't just move from Step V: Brainstorming, or the generation of creative ideas and options, right to Step VII: A Mutual Agreement. We create bridges over which to cross to reach the final step. The bridges are the "supposals and proposals," or Step VI: Agreement Building—Supposals and Proposals.

The "supposal" in the case of "Where do we take our vacation this year?" was a bridge Laura made—going to Mount Katahdin lodge, with Hannah and Abe attending the Eco-Lodge Camp for children. Caleb was still "supposing" that he would be on Martha's Vineyard to rest for two weeks and that Laura would bring the children there for the second week.

Then suddenly Caleb saw a new angle in securing eco-green ideas for his job at the environmental camp. If he could go to a man cave for two to three days to relax, tent, fish, cook outside, and contemplate the moon, with the children not disturbing him too much after their camp, he would go to the Eco-Lodge. It was an *offer*, a *proposal* stronger than a supposal that Caleb made to Laura.

These very same Seven Visual Steps to Yes, illustrated in chapter 3, have been applied to all manner of conflicts and decisions. It works. It helps most pairs make decisions and resolve conflicts and problems. I have used it for many diverse situations in family and divorce mediation and in couples and family mediation.

Who will cook and who will clean up after dinner is a major cause of conflict in many, or shall we say, if not in most households? Thirty or forty years later, the struggles over this conflict may still continue without resolution.

"May I disable your computer monitor to work on my laptop late at night?" "Not unless you reengage it for me to work on in the morning and not leave the cords dangling."

"I want to sell the house at divorce; you want me to stay there until our youngest child graduates from college. I want to move on and this house has bad memories for me."

"I want you to sell one of your houses, so when we get married, we'll be able to buy 'our house' together."

Conflicts are a part of our daily lives because individuals have differing needs, viewpoints, and opinions. So many people are conflict-avoidant or averse. But conflict is natural. It should not be upsetting or an indication that there is a big problem in a relationship, yet it wreaks havoc on our lives unless we have the skills to resolve it. Believe it or not, all of the above conflicts were resolved and decisions made, plus many hundreds more, using the Seven Visual Steps to Yes model.

Many excellent books about conflict and negotiation have been written for business executives and for negotiation between nations. I first began hearing about negotiation and mediation from my readings of Howard Raiffa's *The Art and Science of Negotiation*, the works of Lawrence Susskind at MIT, and Roger Fisher and William Ury's *Getting to Yes* (with Bruce Patton).[3] In *Getting to Yes*, the authors declared they were writing the book expressly for business executives, international diplomats, and business and law students. Along came Herbert Kelman of the Weatherhead Project at Harvard University. Kelman worked with John Burton, a scholar and diplomat from Australia, who also worked at the University of Colorado. The two of them emphasized the importance of the basic human needs concept taken from Abraham Maslow. After delving into negotiation through reading, I attended the Harvard Negotiation Project for training in 1981. The approach was geared mainly, over the years, to the business executive and the international diplomat. I helped cofound the Massachusetts Council on Family Mediation (MCFM), in 1982, which continues to provide education to family and divorce mediators on an alternate month basis.

I stood on the shoulders of the negotiation giants who created and adapted the four-step, principled Getting to Yes approach and the Mutual Gains Approach (MGA) at MIT. As you have seen in this chapter, I made these approaches graphic and easy to understand and use for non-academics and people who aren't business executives or international diplomats. After I added and emphasized steps, I started using this approach with my clients in the office and teaching it to graduate students who helped refine it. The supposals and proposals of Step VI, Agreement Building, are similar to the "what if" step in the Mutual Gains Approach. You will see how rich, textured, scientific, rational, and creative the model is as we go through numerous examples- the case studies in the chapters- that you may well have encountered in your lives.

We all need to know the Seven Visual Steps to Yes. For those of us who already know the method, we need to remember that we know it and apply it.

CHAPTER 5
Sophie and Seth Work toward a Creative Separation

What could be more important than having available to us the Seven Visual Steps to Yes model in our everyday dealings with one another as couples and as families in the resolution of our conflicts and problems and in the making of our decisions?

As I've made clear, the negotiation approaches upon which I have built the Seven Visual Steps to Yes model—the Getting to Yes, Mutual Gains, and *The Art and Science of Negotiation* approaches—are largely oriented toward business executives and international diplomats, and are used in case studies at business and law schools and for academics to talk to one another. The seven-step model is for all of us, especially couples and partners in love relationships, roommates, condo owners, family business owners, ministers and associate ministers, rabbis, their associates and the like.

Sophie and Seth were not just a typical or ordinary couple, nor were they business executives or international diplomats. They were extremely conscientious, dedicated parents, who were involved in their church and in an "ethical humanist" society. In fact, they met at a Society for Ethical Humanists at Boston University. They sensed and then learned that they had been brought up with similar values and beliefs to an extraordinary degree and that they practiced their values in their professions and personal lives. Everything clicked, and soon they and their families joined for an incredibly beautiful and meaningful wedding ceremony on the Delaware coast. Not long afterward Jennifer, an adorable baby girl, was born. Then twins, Adriana and Kathryn, came along to bless their home. Both Sophie and Seth's parents were young grandparents, adored their grandchildren, and contributed time and financial resources to help their adult children. Sophie and Seth did not have to sacrifice their couple relationship to be parents.

This couple and their family were the envy of their friends and acquaintances. Initially, the family occupied a whole pew of little girls with hair ribbons and patent leather shoes, and then they became beautiful, robust, dark-haired adolescents. Each family member found his and her path to the observance of a special kind of spiritual meditation. Almost unbelievably, Seth's company allowed him—with him paying the tab, of course—to take the whole family on trips with him to cosmopolitan urban centers and places with idyllic natural settings.

Neither their colleagues nor their friends nor their parents ever would have detected a fault line in their relationship. Yet here they were in the office asking for decision-making mediation to decide the future of their relationship! Unbelievable. No one would have guessed it. Had they experienced too good a life and now were stretching for even more? They had undergone multiple rounds of intensive couples and individual therapy over a long period of time. After I obtained background information pertaining to their individual lives and couple relationship, the Seven Visual Steps to Yes would be used to achieve a sane, carefully thought-out decision regarding a vision for a marital separation. At all times they were asked to step into the other's shoes and to empathize with what the other must be feeling. The definition of the decision they wanted to reach was "We want to uncover a mutual definition of what we want to achieve, to create, and to deliberately discover during a six-month separation period living apart." They wanted to live deliberatively during the separation period "to find and hold on to ourselves as individuals, not just as family members." They wanted to discover, when they arrived at the end of their allotted period, what they had purposefully visualized and desired to accomplish during their separation.

Sophie brought in a quote from Henry David Thoreau: "I went to the woods because I wished to live deliberately, to front only the essential facts of life, and see if I could not learn what it had to teach, and not, when I came to die, to discover that I had not lived. I did not wish to live what was not life, living is so dear; nor did I wish to practice resignation, unless it was quite necessary. I wanted to live deep and suck out all the marrow of life, to live so sturdily and Spartan-like as to put to rout all that was not life, to cut a broad swath and shave close, to drive life into a corner, and reduce it to its lowest terms."

Seth and Sophie agreed that what Thoreau had said applied to their separation. They did not wish to arrive at the end of the designated time period without having achieved the specific goals they had carved out for their separation. Seth and Sophie were serious and thoughtful people. They wanted a meaningful separation. Using the Seven Visual Steps to Yes model, this time for decision-making rather than conflict resolution, Sophie quickly exclaimed that what she *wanted* during the separation (Step I) was a "pause" in the relationship; Seth said he *wanted* to "restore intimacy to our marriage." It might seem, at the outset that their initial "I want" positions were dissonant or even contradictory. They might well be. But wait a minute. Hundreds of conflicts, problems, or decisions start out this way and end up with jointly satisfying resolutions. Let's look in on Seth and Sophie's seven-step process.

Definition of the Decision to Be Made
How do we create a collaborative vision of our separation?"

Step I: "I " Want" Positions

I want:	Well, I want:
Sophie	Seth

- "a pause in our relationship"
- "to restore intimacy to our marriage"

Step II: My Bottom-Line Need

Sophie	Seth
"freedom"	"home"

Step III: What *Really, Really* Matters to Me

MATTERS TO ME – A SOPHIE	Rate 1-5	MATTERS TO ME – B SETH	Rate 1-5
"To hold on to the better sense of myself I've gained in the last three months"	5	"For me to be committed and open"	5
"Trust and openness"	5	"To have our date nights"	3-4
"I want less pressure in our daily lives."	4	"To take the family trip to New Orleans"	4
"To feel free to say what I *really feel* without Seth taking it personally"	5	"To feel we can both express ourselves freely"	5
"To be a genuine separation, to be able to date and interact with others on all levels, emotionally, spiritually, and physically"	5	"To reconnect to you, Sophie, in every way"	5
"After I've said something, not to hear from Seth that this is not what I really feel"	5	"To be affectionate, have sex, hold hands, kiss, hug"	5

Sophie took more time to articulate what really mattered to her than she had taken to speak about what she wanted and what she needed as her bottom-line need. Seth had an even more difficult time. He rolled his eyes up into his head until he connected with what *really* was important, what *really* mattered to him. When asked, they both said they really did understand what was important to the other one.

Step IV: Best Personal Alternative

This concept is a challenge for most people to grasp. It is difficult to discover or uncover what their safety net is, what they would or could do if they can't achieve a negotiated settlement with the other party. But Sophie and Seth were sophisticated and intelligent, and they held their best alternatives close to their chests, not sharing them aloud. Sophie said her best personal alternative scared her. Seth was more guarded. It turned out that Sophie's best alternative was to step outside the marriage literally and Seth's was to step outside the marriage visually.

Step V: Brainstorming

	BRAINSTORMING CREATIVE OPTIONS and IDEAS	Sophie	Seth
1.	Sophie: "I am more committed to "nesting" with you, living in the home half-time, after having heard how important "home" is to you as what you bottom-line need."	5	5
2.	Sophie: "I will work on being more financially independent, trying to get a second job."	5	5
3.	Seth: "I want intimacy inside the marriage and you want intimacy outside of the marriage."	1	5
4.	Seth: "Fidelity is *huge* for me."	1	5
5.	Seth: "Kissing hello and good-bye for starters, and holding hands."	1	5
6.	Sophie: "Friendship and really good co-parenting."	5	5
7.	Seth: "Family dinners occasionally."	5	5
8.	Seth: "Taking our New Orleans vacation."	4	5
9.	Seth: "In the weeks I am living in the apartment, I will come to the house two evenings a week to have dinner with the girls and to help with their homework."	4	5
10.	Sophie: "Parenting the girls every other day on the weekends."	5	5
11.	Sophie: " Dating and living socially, emotionally, and physically as independent individuals."	5	1

We began the rating process, circling the options that were close and several that were both rated a five, which they knew they would keep as part of their vision for their collaborative separation. I was eager to move them on to Step VI: Agreement Building—Supposals and Proposals, but the session time was up and they both needed to get their daughters to their activities. I sensed they knew they were getting close to the termination of their process.

When they arrived for the next session, Seth's and Sophie's faces were long and drawn. They said they had agreed at home on all of the proposed items that were fives and four to fives, and they would carry them out during a marital separation while living apart. These items had to do with how they would parent their children. But they had also decided to divorce. They could see that what each of them fundamentally needed and what was important to each of them were at cross-purposes. Seth made a supposal that they begin divorce mediation in the next several weeks. Sophie proposed that I give them names of respected mediators within their geographic area. They both said it was unbelievable how doing the Seven Visual Steps to Yes, which they hadn't even completed, brought into clear perspective for both of them that their fundamental, non-negotiable needs were not compatible.

Step VI: Agreement Building—Supposals and Proposals
- **Seth's supposal:** that they begin divorce mediation in the next few weeks.
- **Sophie's supposal:** that I give them recommendations for respected divorce mediators in their geographic area.

Step VII: A Mutual Agreement

> Our basic needs and what really matters to each of us are so very different that we need a divorce, not just a collaborative separation.
>
> *Peace Begins with Us*

As usual with this process, Seth and Sophie were in awe with regard to how simple the Seven Visual Steps to Yes process had worked. To divorce was a lifetime decision for them and for their three children. They were making a carefully thought-out decision about the future direction of not only their own lives but also their children's lives. The two of them were deeply spiritual and ethical people, valuing respect, love, kindness, compassion, and reciprocity. They wanted to live those values, especially in one of the most important decisions of their lifetimes. This process gave them a chance to do that.

CHAPTER 6

Anne and Sam
"We Are Going to Kill One Another If We Don't Separate Immediately"

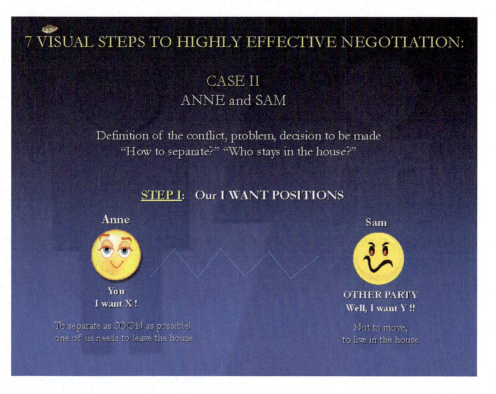

Anne and Sam came in specifically for divorce mediation. They had been attempting to separate for over three years and couldn't decide how they could manage to do so financially. Anne and Sam met in their thirties in the Deep South and had both attended undergraduate and graduate school at Emory University. Their two children were born after they moved to New England while still in their thirties. If you carefully read the charts we made in mediation, presented on the following pages, you will see how they arrived at a conclusion they never thought possible.

STEP II: Your Bottom-line Basic Need:

Anne	Sam
"A HOME"	"THE HOME I DESIGNED"
	(see bottom line needs just below)

STEP III: What *really* matters relative to the conflict. You both will list all your "interests*" and prioritize how much they matter to you

(From Interactive Conflict Resolution)

Examples of Bottom-Line Basic Needs:

- a sense of fairness
- a sense of home
- financial security
- emotional security for me or for me with the children
- a sense of safety
- feeling respected
- feeling recognized
- a sense of freedom
- a sense of autonomy
- confidence in who I am / my identity
- a sense of belongingness
- a sense of love
- something else

Anne	#	Sam	#
Separating SOON	5	Continuity / not moving	5
Having my own home	5	Passing on house I designed to children	5
Having enough money for retirement	5	That children have their familiar home to return to	5
Having enough money to buy my own house	5	That it would be a shame to lose my self-designed house just because I don't have inheritance money yet	5
Having enough money, after house and personal expenses to share children's graduate school expenses	5		
Sharing our personal effects and household goods equally	5		

* *this step is called "interests" in the M.I.T. and Harvard models of "Mutual Gains" and "Getting to Yes"*

Janet Miller Wiseman's 7 VISUAL STEP NEGOTIATION MODEL *(continued)*

STEP IV: My Own Personal Best Alternative
This is your safety net, what you can do all by yourself if you cannot achieve a negotiation settlement with the other party.

STEP V: Brainstorm Creative Alternatives
See definition under Seth and Sophie Case I I Illustration

FACTS	
1.	Living Expenses for the home are $39,000/year
2.	Anne earns $125,000 gross this year
3.	Sam will earn $35,000 gross this year, but has business expenses
4.	Sam will inherit $2.5 million when 93 year old Mom dies
5.	If Anne stayed in home, she would have only $2,500 total/yr after paying taxes, health insurance, retirement and her own expenses.

Brainstorming: Generating Creative Ideas and Options		Anne	Sam
1.	Sam offers: Anne lives in the home until I receive trust money. Mom age 93 has Alzheimer's. Sam is sole beneficiary. Trust is $2.5M	1	Rate 1 – 5 (5 Best) 5
2.	Anne offers: We put the home on the market now	5	1
3.	Sam offers: Anne pays some of my expenses-alimony until I receive my trust money. (We do calculations).	1	5
4.	Sam offers: We buy lottery tickets; purchase and win	1	5
5.	Anne: rent to a third party for price that will make us money until he receives trust when he can buy the home.	1	1
6.	Anne: I have $369,000 in inheritance money. I want to use it for retirement, but could find out if bank would give me a mortgage with my $130,000 income	3	4
7.	Sam: I find out whether 1-2 tenants' rent would provide enough income to stay there until she receives inheritance	3	3
8.	Sam: I'm the trustee of Mom's trust; find out if I can get a management fee for extra income	4	5
9.	Sam: Find out if I can somehow access part of trust funds before Mom dies	2	5

STEP VI: BUILDING AGREEMENT STAGE

Janet Miller Wiseman starts with:

a. SUPPOSALS 1ST: *(copyright 1983)*

"suppose we …" in a negotiation:
" I suppose we …" or "I'd like you each to begin with supposals, which are softer and gentler than a proposal."
(for a Mediator to use)

Anne: We see how much tenant rental(s) would provide. Would they cover Sam's expenses?

Sam: Will do. Did not. "Rentals aren't guaranteed"

Sam: 2nd supposal "You see if you can get a mortgage with the amount of money you have in your inherited account."

Anne: Will do. Did not.

Counter Supposal-Later. Don't want to deplete this account which should be for retirement.

Sam- 3rd supposal: "I'll see if I can get money out of trust before Mom dies.

BUILDING AGREEMENT STAGE *(continued)*

b. **PROPOSALS:**

Janet Miller Wiseman as Mediator … "Now that you have heard each other's supposals; one of you may be ready to make a proposal for solution."

   a. Sam: Since I can't get money out of trust until Mom dies and tenant income is not guaranteed I propose you live in the house until I get my inheritance and can buy you out.

   b. Okay. (Agreement lasted for one day)

   c. Next day she emails and says that this doesn't enable her to make improvements on the house, to have her own house and move on with her life.

   d. Anne says: "We're going to have to sell, unless anyone has any ideas."

   e. Janet Miller Wiseman, mediator: "What if Sam applies for a mortgage with the local bank with his $312,000 in home equity and as sole beneficiary to his Mother's trust?"

   f. Sam: "Credit is so limited. Couldn't happen."

   g. Janet Miller Wiseman: "Don't assume."

   h. Sam goes to the bank. They say "Make an application."

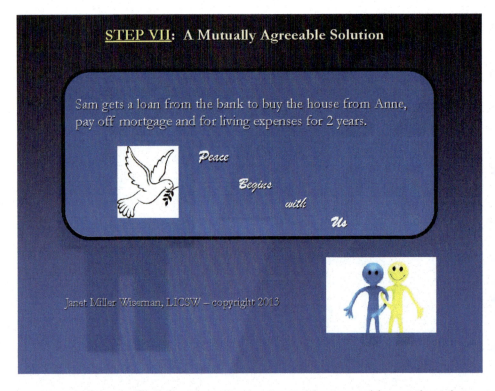

With his half of the equity in the marital home and being the sole heir to his mother's trust, Sam's long-term bank was willing to make him a loan. The loan would enable him to buy out Anne's interest in the home and provide some monies for the next two years before he would receive Social Security payments to supplement his income. Anne would pay some alimony for two years until Sam received Social Security, and she would use the money she received from the buyout of the marital home for a substantial down payment on a condominium and keep her inheritance account in place for retirement. Theirs was a creative, out-of-the-box solution. No wonder this couple had a difficult time seeing possibilities for who could buy out whom in order to effectuate a resolution to their marital settlement.

CHAPTER 7
The Importance of Step II: Bottom-Line Basic Human Needs

You've seen four examples of the use of the Seven Visual Steps to Yes model: the conflict between Adnan and Sherrie about building an addition onto their home for her mother, the conflict between Laura and Caleb about where to go on vacation, the decision to be made by Sophie and Seth regarding their continued separation, and the decision to be made by Anne and Sam regarding who would get the marital home. Which seven steps have impressed you most in terms of their abilities to help parties reach resolution? Or do you think they are all of equal importance?

I used to deeply believe that people's basic human *need* was the most important step (Step II). Most people tell me the whole process (all seven steps) is most important. Someone at the Rhode Island Association of Divorce Mediators, where I was presenting this approach, recently said that the rating system is the most helpful in assisting couples to reach decisions or resolve conflicts. Someone else at the Massachusetts Counsel on Family Mediation agreed that the rating system is most helpful to people making decisions. They see a five across from a zero. That option is not going to be chosen for Step VII: A Mutual Agreement. Numbers don't lie. I think this opinion, that the rating system has great merit, as the most important aspect of this model, is correct, but I also emphasize the importance of the basic human needs.

When negotiating the collective vision of their separation, our case in chapter 3, I could see on Sophie's face, as clearly as suddenly turning on a light bulb, that she deeply understood the importance of Seth's being in and surrounded by "home," his basic human need. I'd guess that to Seth "home" meant a sense of belonging to a family unit, being connected to his three children, being close to the rhythm of daily life, as well as being the main financial provider at that time. Sophie had "gotten it" with Seth's expression in Step II that home was his bottom-line basic need. She accommodated Seth's need, even though that would make her own life incredibly more complicated. She would have to return home on the week she had off from caretaking to be there with the children until Seth returned home. The couple had decided to parent the children every other week in their home. Obviously she would get involved in cleaning, laundry, and straightening while she was there for her week. Likewise, although Sophie had said she wanted "freedom" many times before, by saying it in the context of a basic human need, Seth got it and said he truly wanted her to feel free and not hemmed in, as long as she didn't take it too far. He said that her feelings of freedom were in his best interest in the marriage.

In the case of Liz and Doug, they were ahead of Seth and Sophie in knowing that they were going to divorce. Liz and Doug, a couple in their thirties with two young children, had come to the office for divorce mediation. After preliminary instructions for the process of divorce mediation, Doug said he needed immediate help with Liz whom he labeled as attempting to control him, even though she did not want to be married to him. He said, "She just can't have it both ways: throw me out and reel me in!" She was trying to set restrictions on his going out to restaurant-bars in the evenings to hear music with his friends. Liz was struggling to find words to explain her behavior when I asked if she was concerned that the community would see Doug out with the guys before their divorce and conclude he was "available," searching for someone new, or maybe, that an affair was contributing to their divorce. Liz acknowledged that this was her reservation, but she did not understand why this was bothering her so much. When asked if she was dating, she said she believed that would be "disrespectful" and "immoral" until the couple was actually divorced. When I asked Doug if he was searching for a sense of "belonging," no longer having a mate or a home that would be his, Doug concurred. A sense of belonging is a very important human need. They agreed that Liz would feel more comfortable if Doug wore his wedding ring until the court date and be clear with his buddies and women at restaurants and bars that he was separated, not dating, and not yet available.

After having heard the words "respect" and "belonging"—without even spelling out to Liz and Doug that these were basic human needs—both of them appeared comfortable with their mutual agreement to wear their wedding rings until the court date. Respect, for Liz, and belonging, for Doug, were their bottom-line basic needs (Step II).

Addressing basic human needs is extremely important in virtually every negotiation or in making virtually every decision. As another example, Ileana was boiling over with rage when she and Eric came into the office last summer. She was almost out of control. I was honestly fearful that she might hit Eric. The couple was not married and never planned to be. Eric lived in the southern part of the country, employed as the manager of a large chain of bookstores. Ileana worked almost full-time as an executive administrative assistant and was taking care of their 1½-year-old son, Daniel, with the help of her mother, sister, and some part-time paid help. Eric had another son, who lived in another part of the United States with his mother, whom Eric had also never married. Ileana had taken Daniel to see Eric, but other than these times, Eric had not reached out to see his son. Ileana was furious. She believed that Daniel had a right to know his dad. Furthermore, she believed Daniel had a right to receive child support from his father. Her anger was so intense that it was difficult for us to have a constructive discussion. Suddenly I tried to imagine her basic, bottom-line need. I asked

Ileana if she wanted recognition and respect for making efforts—with her own financial resources and without child support from Eric—to unite father and son. She immediately calmed down, grateful, I believe, that her efforts to unite father and son had been openly acknowledged and recognized. We continued the session without her outbursts.

The power of representing oneself or having someone else recognize what one fundamentally needs—Step II: My Bottom-Line Need—is not to be underestimated. Herbert Kelman at Harvard University's Weatherhead Center, and Australian scholar and diplomat John Burton suggested that the "needs" concept was more appropriately used in international negotiation than in the Getting to Yes settlement model, which is most frequently used in business negotiations. For decades I have included basic, bottom-line human needs as Step II in the Seven Visual Steps to Yes model of negotiation. The basic bottom-line need is necessary for the other party to know in any negotiation or in making any decision. Remember when Sophie and Seth were using the model to create a mutual vision for their separation? As we stated before, after Sophie heard that Seth's basic bottom-line need was "home," she included, in the creative options for the separation, a commitment to each live in the home for one week and in "the apartment" for one week—the "nesting" living arrangement—even though that option would be much more difficult for her. She was willing to suggest the nesting arrangement because she heard how vital home was to Seth when he expressed his basic, bottom-line human need. Seth wanted a sense of intimacy in his marriage; he needed a sense of home.

Just as Abraham Maslow's original hierarchy of human needs began with a five-stage model without a visual pyramid (see Maslow's model below), my Seven Visual Steps to Yes model for effective negotiation began with the MIT Mutual Gains Approach and the Harvard Program on Negotiation's Getting to Yes principled negotiation approach. I changed the names of the steps to be somewhat more understandable to people in my office; added basic bottom-line needs, supposals, and proposals; and made the approach visual. I have offered specific cases to illustrate the Seven Visual Steps to Yes approach to make it easier for people to remember the steps.

Abraham Maslow's Hierarchy of Human Needs

Abraham Maslow's original hierarchy of human needs, developed between 1943 and 1954, was first published in his book *Motivation and Personality*. As seen in the illustration, this original version for most people remains the definitive "hierarchy of needs." Maslow did not use a pyramid, which is depicted in the illustration.

1. Biological and physiological needs. Basic life needs--air, food, drink, shelter, warmth, sex, sleep, etc.

2. Safety needs -- protection, security, order, law, limits, stability, etc.

3. Belonging and love needs -- family, affection, relationships, work group, etc.

4. Esteem needs --achievement, status, responsibility, reputation

5. Self-actualization -- personal growth and fulfillment

```
                        /\
                       /  \
                      /    \
                     /      \
                    /        \
                   / 6: Knowledge and meaning \
                  /    or cognitive needs      \
                 /                              \
                / 7: Aesthetic needs, appreciation and search for \
               /         beauty, balance and form                  \
              /                                                     \
             / 8: Transcendence; helping others to achieve self-actualization \
            /                                                                  \
           / 9: The need for spirituality or seeking something higher than one's own ego \
          /_____\
```

In the 1970s Maslow's hierarchy of human needs was adapted to add "self-actualization- seeking personal growth and peak experiences." One could argue that most people on earth do not have the opportunity to achieve self-actualization, let alone call it a "need" or "basic human need." Maslow's hierarchy at that time put "knowledge and meaning or cognitive needs" in fifth place, instead of self-actualization, and added "aesthetic needs or appreciation and search for beauty, balance, and form" as number six. Knowledge and meaning or cognitive needs are perhaps basic human needs for the self-actualized person in modern, industrialized societies, but they are not basic human needs in most of the world.

In the 1990s an anonymous person added, as number eight in the hierarchy of human needs, the concept of transcendence or "helping others to achieve self-actualization." It has been said that the first four of Maslow's needs are "deficiency motivators" and that numbers six through eight are "growth" motivators that most people on earth at this time will not achieve. A colleague of mine, Susan Kulton Sylva, has suggested a ninth need: "the need for spirituality or seeking something higher than one's own ego." That need and its fulfillment certainly does not require living in an advanced, developed country. Research has shown that the average rickshaw puller in India is as happy as the average American. One might guess that he lives in the moment and might seek something higher than his own ego, a spiritual need.

What happened with Maslow's Hierarchy of human needs is what I have done with MIT and Harvard University's models of negotiation. I have adapted and added to the Mutual Gains Approach and the Getting to Yes models and created the Seven Visual Steps to Yes that I use in my office and hope, by means of this book, will be available to as many couples, partners, children, families, college students, church and temple personnel, and community organizations as possible.

CHAPTER 8
"Compromise" Does Not Belong in the Seven Visual Steps to Yes

Many people, even Webster's dictionary, think of compromise as "meeting in the middle," *giving up some of what you want* to get other things you want. But is that what we're striving for in our negotiation/decision-making/problem-solving method? Is compromise what we mean when we say "mutually agreeable solution"? Would you be surprised if I said "Absolutely not!"? We are *not* aiming to have either party give up what he or she wants, or to give in to what the other wants. We want both parties to achieve their fundamental bottom-line basic need. Caleb achieved two weeks of rest, and Laura hiked at Mount Katahdin, spread her father's ashes, and lost weight to boot. Anne achieved a home to call her own, and Sam received continuity, along with the house he'd designed to pass along to his children. From the beginning of their process, it was clear that Sophie and Seth were far apart on what they wanted during the separation for themselves but absolutely together on what both wanted for their children.

A couple may be arguing about something that, in the scheme of things, may be relatively minor, such as which film to see this evening. If the husband rather fiercely wants to see *The Imitation Game*, about Alan Turing decoding an enigma during World War II, and the wife has her heart set on seeing *Still Alice*, about a woman with Alzheimer's disease, and they both move to the middle to "compromise" about what they will see, they mostly likely will end up seeing something neither one of them likes and neither one is dying to see.

A compromise could be seeing the films they each want to see at different times, or going to a cinema complex where both films were playing and each viewing a separate movie, or seeing both of them in one night. Another option would be to rent both movies "on demand" on television or wait until they come out on Netflix. In this alternative, the couple could use the Seven Visual Steps to Yes model to hear what matters to the other, their basic human needs for that night. They could generate some options to see if they could arrive at one film that would be really satisfying to both of them.

Each time you try this process and succeed, you gain more confidence in your abilities to achieve what you both want, to quit fighting, and to cease being passively aggressive and "compromising," achieving an outcome that neither of you really wants. This mutually satisfying agreement is called in other models of negotiation a "win-win solution."

CHAPTER 9
"I'm Pregnant … and …"

"I'm pregnant," James heard Gretchen say when she called him at the church where he was lead minister. "Oh, happy day," James sang out. "It's been seven years we've been trying and finally it has happened!" Gretchen asked, "Can you come home?" Could he come home? He promised Gretchen he'd be there as soon as he could without getting a speeding ticket. Gretchen was sobbing when James arrived in the front hallway. What could possibly be wrong? Were there problems with the pregnancy, or had changes in hormones already resulted in fits of moodiness?

"I have no idea why I did it!" Gretchen kept repeating between sobs. "Did what?" James thought. Finally Gretchen's sobbing quieted enough for her to share with James that the baby might not be his. In his delirium, it crossed James's mind that Gretchen might have secretly had a sperm donor for an in vitro fertilization. She wanted a child so much. Was that even possible? And could she have done that without consulting him? She wouldn't have. She couldn't have. When asked, Gretchen answered, "Of course not! I'm more ethical than that—at least in some ways!" James was getting more confused. Gretchen then blurted out that she had been having an affair with Joe, the general contractor for their home renovations since shortly after the work began.

Although this revelation put some puzzle pieces together, James was devastated, humiliated, embarrassed, insecure, and angry. But at least Gretchen had been able to conceive a baby, regardless of who the father was. After seven years of attempting to conceive, that was a relief of sorts. Gretchen had wanted to be a mother since she was a small girl, and they both wanted a child. But what to do now? Intellectually, James already knew that he could forgive Gretchen if she wanted to preserve the marriage, and he would want to keep the baby. But what if the baby looked like dark-skinned Joe, a Mediterranean, and not like Gretchen and him, both hailing from somewhat medium-skin-toned families? Tongues would wag immediately, especially in the church congregation. It was none of their business! Intermittently, James and Gretchen sat together to ponder their situation thoughtfully, interspersed with bouts of intense anger and recrimination. Gretchen accused the church and its congregation of being James's mistresses, leaving her alone and emotionally bereft. They pondered and fought until they knew for sure that time was running out to make a responsible decision about how to go forward.

When they came into the office this spring, James quickly presented that Gretchen was pregnant and didn't know if he was the father; the baby may have been fathered by the general contractor of their home renovations. He was not exactly in favor of, but was pondering abortion. Aha, Step I was presented without even asking for it! Gretchen was quietly crying, "I want us to have this child. She may be the biological child of both of us." Gretchen also knew her "I Want" position.

Step I: "I Want" Positions

I want: | **I want:**
Gretchen | **James**

- "To have this baby"
- "I want a child but wonder about abortion this time around."

Step II: My Bottom-Line Need

As mediator, I asked them their bottom-line basic needs. "To be a father," James answered. "To be a mother," Gretchen answered.

Step III: What *Really, Really* Matters to Me
What really matters in this negotiation and how important each item is (1–5)

MATTERS TO ME – A GRETCHEN	Rate 1-5	MATTERS TO ME – B JAMES	Rate 1-5
"Not to abort this baby; I may never get pregnant again."	5	"Not to jeopardize my career and potential to provide for my family."	5
"To be a mother."	5	"Not to be a negative role model as a minister."	5
"Not to be embarrassed."	5	"Not to have to make explanations to higher-up authorities in the church hierarchy or to members of my church family."	4
"Not to lose this baby."	5	"Having a happy marriage."	5
"Not to lose James."	5	"Living my values."	5
		"My own credibility and truthfulness."	5
		"To be a father."	5

When asked if they could stand in the other's shoes and empathize with what was truly important to the other, they each said that they absolutely could.

Step IV: Best Personal Alternative

This step may not always be shared with the other party until after the negotiation.. When I asked each of them later what their best personal alternatives had been in order to know how this step had influenced reaching their mutual agreement, James' best alternative was to have the baby, stay together, and request a transfer of his ministerial post to another district out of state. Gretchen's best alternative was, if James did not want to stay with her and if the baby was Joe's, to file for child support from Joe and move to North Carolina to be near her family. These alternatives, of course, were safety nets if they could not reach a mutual agreement.

Step V: Brainstorming

	BRAINSTORMING CREATIVE OPTIONS and IDEAS	Gretchen	James
1.	Gretchen: "The baby could be James' biological child. I'll stay here. James undergoes a process to forgive me. I undergo a process to forgive myself, and we're relieved to have our child after seven years of waiting."	5	4
2.	Gretchen: "If the baby is not James', I could get child support from Joe, move back to North Carolina, give the church some excuse if James does not want to stay married to me. I feel so guilty."	1	2
3.	Gretchen: "We could divorce if James doesn't want to stay with me."	4	2
4.	Gretchen: "If the baby is ours and we're divorced, we'd both have joint custody and an equal part in bringing 'her' up."	3	5
5.	Gretchen: "If the baby is not yours James, and you want a divorce, you wouldn't have to stay involved in the baby's life."	5	4
6.	James: "Maybe think about having an abortion?"	2	5
7.	James: "After having a DNA test, if the baby isn't mine, put him/her up for an open adoption and Gretchen could see the baby and be an 'auntie' in the baby's life."	2	5
8.	James: "Tell church members the baby was born with *major* birth defects and is being adopted by a family that has adopted similar babies in the past." (Gretchen rolls her eyes...)	1	1

James and Gretchen had vented a good deal of feeling while creating options.

Step VI: Agreement Building—Supposals and Proposals

- James supposed: "Gretchen, suppose we see how early we can get a DNA test to determine the paternity of the child?"
- Gretchen counter-supposed: "I disagree. I think we should *not* have a DNA test and just assume the baby is our baby, spiritually."
- Gretchen: "If the DNA test shows the baby is not yours, James, and you don't want to be married to me, I can move back to North Carolina."
- "Hey, Gretch, let's arrange that you are in North Carolina at about the due date, which no one else needs to know for sure. You deliver down there. If the baby is not mine or really, really doesn't look like me, you stay there for a while, due to some delivery difficulties. I'll start putting in applications now for transfer of pulpit to other places in the country."
- "Yes," Gretchen echoes, "and if the baby is ours, we don't have to take a transfer. But this seems so unethical to play around with the church's time to process your applications and interview you, just because I made a mistake."
- James then proposes that he request an administrative post in the same church in the administrative headquarters downtown, in another location within the same city, and they buy a home in another suburb within the same city.
- Gretchen keeps insisting that James is making all the concessions and that she made the mistake. He keeps insisting that they both equally want a child and that this is better than adoption because, in the worst-case scenario, the baby will have half of their genes. He has totally given up the option of an abortion.
- Tell people the baby is being adopted by a family that has

adopted babies with major birth defects, such as their baby has. (Gretchen thinks, "Since when do ministers lie?" and James thinks, "Since when do ministers' wives have affairs?" as they roll their eyes.)
- James' final proposal, which became their mutual agreement, was: "Let's not find out who the biological father is for some time and let people assume, if she or he is dark-skinned, that we had artificial insemination. We won't have to move or get a new job. We will be just fine with *our* new baby."

Step VII: A Mutual Agreement

> Let's not even find out for a while who is the biological father. Whatever the baby looks like, he or she will be ours. We could have received artificial insemination, so people can simply assume that. We won't have to move or get a new job. We will be just fine with "our" new baby!
>
> *Peace Begins with Us*

Long after the DNA testing, Gretchen and James reported that their daughter had Joe's DNA but looked very much like both of them. Several years later, Gretchen and James came to the office with two-year-old Kathryn. Although she had proven to have been biologically Joe's child, in every other way she was their child using their gestures, mannerisms, and tone of voice. Gretchen had entered individual therapy to understand on a deep level the roots of her need for the affair. James was in a similar forum to deal with the hurt and anger that the affair had caused him, and they continued their forum here, transforming it from a decision-making intervention into a relationship-strengthening intervention.

About seven other couples have come to my office over the last forty some years with similar situations of a pregnancy in which the father might not be the biological father of the child. They have not all had outcomes similar to that of James and Gretchen in which they have happily stayed together. Indeed, a greater proportion of these cases, in which the seven-step model was not used, have divorced. I have wondered whether some of the marriages that ended in divorce might not have derailed if they had used the Seven Visual Steps to Yes model.

CHAPTER 10
"She's Not Pregnant ... but ..."

Unlike Gretchen and James, more couples present with one of them having had an affair but without a baby involved. Either a spouse finds something to indicate an infidelity or a spouse decides, for one reason or another, to tell his or her partner about the affair. The apparent sense of betrayal—having been lied to, sometimes for a very long time, and feeling hurt and angry—looks and feels to the partner, and to an outsider, almost equally as devastating as one in which a child has been conceived.

One example, of many, was Neil and Ceci, empty nesters with a variety of individual interests. Neil was a successful writer and competitive bicyclist who also played doubles tennis twice a week and swam. Ceci, an accomplished weaver, had a retail shop where she sold antiques and her weavings, along with her paintings and other artists' crafts. Ceci discovered that Neil had been having an affair with his tennis partner of two years, Cynthia. Ceci had the telephone receiver in her hand, ready to call Cynthia's husband, Craig, to inform him of the affair when something told her to wait. She wanted to enlist Craig's help to stop this nonsense immediately, and she wanted to shame Neil, but she especially wanted to shame Cynthia. "For God's sake, Cynthia, what do you think you are doing with *my* husband?" she wanted to scream. She was outraged, but her feelings were directed more toward Cynthia than toward Neil. If she could humiliate, hurt, and shame Cynthia profoundly, that wouldn't be enough!

When they got to my office, Neil begged Ceci not to call Cynthia's husband, Craig. Neil did not want Craig to even contemplate divorcing Cynthia, who didn't want a divorce and who could not take care of herself financially. We slowly proceeded through the Seven

Visual Steps to Yes model several times, and at several stages, over the two years it took for them to talk, forgive, heal, and find their way forward.

Definition of the Issue
"How can we heal from Neil's affair and get back to a new normal?"

Step I: "I Want" Positions

I want: Ceci	I want: Neil

- "I want you to never see Cynthia again!"
- "Get a new tennis partner!"

- "I want to respectfully let Cynthia know our romance is over and probably our friendship as well."

Step II: Bottom-Line Need

Ceci
- To be convinced of your lifelong love for me
- To understand how I failed to meet your needs, Neil

Neil
- For you to acknowledge that your intense involvement with your store and women's group left me lonely and vulnerable to an affair

Step III: What *Really, Really* Matters to Me

MATTERS TO ME – A CECI	Rate 1-5	MATTERS TO ME – B NEIL	Rate 1-5
"Knowing how many people know about this affair."	5	"For you not to talk with Cynthia's husband, Craig."	5
"Being assured that this affair will end *immediately*!"	5	"Give me a few weeks to find a new tennis league and a new tennis partner."	5
"Being assured you won't see Cynthia again."	5	"Begin couples therapy with me. I want you to understand how intensely lonely I was with you all wrapped up in your store and your women's group."	5
"Being assured that Neil will get a new tennis league and a new tennis partner tomorrow."	4	"Give me a chance to make up the betrayal to you."	5
"I may want to talk with Cynthia's husband, Craig."	4	"I need you to understand how empty I felt when the children left for college. We can talk about this in therapy."	5

Step IV: Best Personal Alternative

As usual, the partners were asked to think about what their best personal alternative would be if they couldn't reach a settlement with the other party and to keep this answer to themselves unless they were very good alternatives. When I asked them, long after the negotiation, Neil and Ceci both said they would spend time apart so their spouse could see how much he or she appreciated the other. Neil was thinking of spending six months apart; Ceci was thinking of three months.

Step V: Brainstorming

	BRAINSTORMING CREATIVE OPTIONS and IDEAS	Ceci	Neil
1.	Ceci: "Spending time exploring what our individual life missions are, our goals and needs as individuals and as a couple."	5	5
2.	Neil: "Spending time exploring what our unmet longings are as individuals and as a couple."	5	5
3.	Ceci: "Exploring what we can't tolerate in a marriage, such as betrayal, lack of trust, and infidelity."	5	5
4.	Neil: "Going back in time to explore how we each were feeling as the children left for college."	5	5
5.	Ceci: "Talking about the differences in our cultural backgrounds: especially the messages we received about the expression of affection and sexuality in a couple."	5	5
6.	Neil: "Going back in time to explore how I felt when you were intensely involved with your store and your women's group."	5	5

Step VI: Agreement Building—Supposals and Proposals

- Neil made a supposal that they combine all of the options and more in an extended contract or in "relationship-strengthening mediation."
- Ceci agreed with Neil's supposal, but, as a counter-supposal, she first might have to talk with Cynthia to tell her to "lay off my husband."
- Neil proposed that he would change tennis partners and leagues and explain the new situation to Cynthia, telling her he wouldn't be in contact with her under any circumstances. In turn, Ceci would have to give him more time than "immediately" to do so.
- Ceci proposed that Neil have a week to explain the situation to

Cynthia, which she thought was very generous indeed.
- Neil counter-proposed that he have a month to detach from Cynthia and explain the situation to her.
- "Out of the question," Cynthia bellowed. "Do you take me for a fool?"
- "Okay, then three weeks," countered Neil.
- "No!" countered Ceci, "not a minute more than two weeks, starting this minute!"
- Neil agreed and they had mutual agreement, the final step of the Seven Visual Steps to Yes.

Step VII: A Mutual Agreement

> We'll continue working here in couples mediation to understand ourselves as individuals and as a couple. We will learn to forgive, attempt to heal, and the relationship with the "intruder" will be terminated. We will concentrate on making our relationship fun and joyous. Neil will end the relationship with Cynthia within two weeks.
>
> *Peace Begins with Us*

Ceci and Neil reviewed, within their couples mediation, the next stage after decision making mediation, the center stage that raising their children had taken in their marriage, and the meaning the children's growing up and leaving home had meant to both of them, but especially to Neil. They talked about the emptiness he felt with the children leaving home for university and the vulnerability he felt to having the affair while Ceci was deeply occupied with her store and her women's group. Ceci could see that she bore some responsibility for Neil's involvement with Cynthia and began a slow process of forgiveness. The couple did separate for four months but found that they were eating at each other's residence and sleeping over so much that it was clear how much they were enjoying one another and their newfound empty nest. They found their way back to the marriage, but it wasn't without two solid years in couple's mediation.

CHAPTER 11

Bill and Sally's Divorce: Sally Wants Not to Be a Bag Lady; Bill Wants a Fair Share

Using the Financial Specialist, CDFA, CFP to Help Clients Feel Secure About the Longevity of their Assets

In addition to Anne and Sam, in order to demonstrate the use of the Seven Visual Steps to Yes we look in on Bill and Sally, another couple who came into the office for divorce mediation. Now in their early fifties, they had met at the University of Virginia, married in their senior year, and entered the Peace Corps, serving in Zimbabwe shortly after their college graduations. When asked what each wanted, Sally immediately chimed in, "I want to be okay. I want to feel secure and safe that I am doing the right thing financially without Bill at my side." Bill said he wanted a fair and reasonable division of their assets. He had started and later sold a start-up software company that refined and further developed the robotic arm used in surgery. Both he and Sally felt instinctively that the sale of the assets worth $5.2 million would last them the rest of their lives without working. They immediately responded yes when I spoke about bringing in a financial specialist, Chris Chen, a certified divorce and financial analyst (CDFA), to one or several sessions to do calculations to be sure that their instincts were correct.

Bill and Sally saw this time in their lives as time to "give back," neither one desiring to be tied to the need to earn future money, except with activities that brought them happiness and/or gave back to the community.

7 VISUAL STEPS TO HIGHLY EFFECTIVE NEGOTIATION:

CASE III
Bill and Sally

Definition of issue:
"We want a fair division of our assets"

STEP I: Your "I WANT" POSITIONS
Each person states his/her initial position
"I want out completely"

Sally   Bill

You   OTHER PARTY
I want X !   Well, I want Y !!

To be sure I'm going   To have a fair division
to be okay financially   of our assets

"NO BAG LADY FOR ME! & I WANT MY FAIR SHARE"

STEP II: Your Bottom-line Basic Need:

Sally	Bill
"Financial Security & Safety"	"Financial Security"

STEP III: What _really_ matters relative to the conflict. You both will list all your "interests*" and prioritize how much they matter to you

(From Interactive Conflict Resolution)

Sally	#	Bill	#
Sense of Safety	5	A fair and reasonable division of assets	4/5
To stay in the house if it makes financial sense	5	To keep some mutual funds parents started for me as a child	5
Not to have to work to make a lot of money	5	To live within my means without having to work i.e. start another company	4/5
To have a familiar place for our daughter to come home from college	4/5	To rent or buy another house below costs that I could "afford"	5
To feel that I am making the wisest choices for me now that Bill won't be around to guide me at all times.	5		

Examples of Bottom-Line Basic Needs:

- a sense of fairness
- a sense of home
- financial security
- emotional security for me or for me with the children
- a sense of safety
- feeling respected
- feeling recognized
- a sense of freedom
- a sense of autonomy
- confidence in who I am / my identity
- a sense of belongingness
- a sense of love
- something else

* _this step is called "interests" in the M.I.T. and Harvard models of "Mutual Gains" and "Getting to Yes"_

Janet Miller Wiseman's 7 VISUAL STEP NEGOTIATION MODEL *(continued)*

STEP IV: Your Personal Best Alternative
This is your safety net, what you can do all by yourself if you cannot achieve a negotiation settlement with the other party.

STEP V: Generate Creative Options by Brainstorming
Together, you can both suggest sane AND wild ideas for resolving the conflict or solving the problem. Do not eliminate any idea that comes to mind. Rate the ideas/options. Each party gives each idea/option a number from 1 to 5 to indicate how desirable that idea/option is to him/her. Each party or the Mediator circles the options which get the highest ratings from each of the parties and are closest to 5's. The other ideas are eliminated.

Creative Brainstorming		Sally	Bill
1.	JMW Bring financial specialist (CFA,CDFA) into session to calculate longevity of dividends on mutual funds if Sally retains house	Rate 1 – 5 (5 Best) 5	5
2.	Sally offers: Split all mutual funds equally after she keeps house if she'll have enough funds after that	5	5
3.	Bill offers: Also split retirement and invested funds, indeed most all assets	5	5
4.	Bill offers: He keeps money given to him by parents as a child	5	5
5.	Sally and Bill: We waive alimony one from the other in the future	5	5

STEP VI: AGREEMENT STAGE

Janet Miller Wiseman starts with:

a. **SUPPOSALS:** *(copyright 1983)*
   " suppose we ..." in a negotiation:

   " I suppose we ..." or "I'd like you each to begin with supposals, which are softer and gentler than a proposal."
   (for a Mediator to use)

   Sally comes back from mediation friendly review attorney supposing we leave alimony open for 8 years after divorce if either of them is making more than $150,000/year.

b. **PROPOSALS:**

   Janet Miller Wiseman as Mediator ...
   "Now that you have heard each other's supposals; one of you may be ready to make a proposal for solution."

   c. Modifications, counter-supposals and counter-proposals:
      "I'd like to modify that by ... "

   d. Combining Options: Bill: I propose we divide all assets 50-50, except I keep the funds from my parents that they started for me as a child. We keep alimony open for 8 years if either of us is making more than $150,000 per year.

   e. "Sounds Great!"

   f. "It's a deal!"

STEP VII: A Mutually Agreeable Solution

Bill and Sally divide all assets 50-50, except Bill keeps the funds from his parents that they started for him as a child. They keep alimony open for 8 years if either of them is making more than $150,000 per year.

Peace

Begins

with

Us

Janet Miller Wiseman, LICSW, 2013

Will Sally be a bag lady?

The Financial Analysis for Sally

Fact Pattern:

- Bill and Sally are 58 years old

- They do not work

- Assets: house, retirement accounts, investment accounts, cash

- Net Worth: $5.2M

- Proposed Asset Split:
  - 50/50
  - Sally keeps the house and 38% of financial assets
  - Bill keeps 62% of financial assets

The CDFA constructed the property division between Bill and Sally, which appears below:

Property Division

	Sally Amount	Pct	Bill Amount	Pct	Total Amount
Real Estate Equity					
Marital Home	$720,000		$0		$720,000
Total Value $720,000					
Equity $720,000					
Cash & Investments					
Fidelity-B	$165,074		$269,330		$434,404
Janus B	$1,000,706		$1,632,732		$2,633,438
Putnam-J	$86,608		$141,307		$227,915
Calvert-J	$49,636		$80,986		$130,622
Calvert-J	$9,987		$16,294		$26,281
Leader-J	$0		$7,648		$7,648
CSB-F	$4,133		$0		$4,133
Total Investments	$1,316,144	38%	$2,148,297	62%	$3,464,441
Cars and Personal Effects					
Other Property	$30,000		$0		$30,000
Other Property	$0		$20,000		$20,000
Total Personal Items	$30,000	60%	$20,000	40%	$50,000
Subtotal Non-Retirement	$2,066,144	49%	$2,168,297	51%	$4,234,441
IRA/401ks					
American Funds IRA	$508,770		$508,769		$1,017,539
ING 403(b)	$2,415		$2,414		$4,829
First Trust IRA	$5,372		$5,372		$10,744
Total IRA/401ks	$516,557	50%	$516,555	50%	$1,033,112
Subtotal Retirement	$516,557	50%	$516,555	50%	$1,033,112
Total Assets	$2,582,701	49%	$2,684,852	51%	$5,267,553

Sally was able to see the pie chart with her share of the house and the mutual funds.

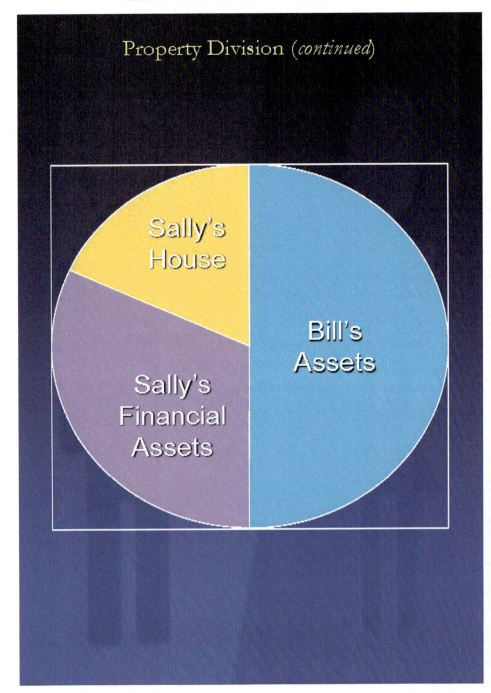

The most helpful for Sally was to face realistically the amount she spends, both fixed expenses and her discretionary expenses each month.

Monthly Living Expenses

Living Expenses	
Homeowners' Insurance	$65.17
Real Estate Tax	562.50
Cable TV	125.00
Phone	95.00
Household Maintenance	218.75
Maid/Cleaning Service	95.00
Lawn Service	116.67
Utilities - Electricity	144.42
Utilities - Gas/Propane Heat	157.92
Utilities - Water/Sewer	255.00
Car Insurance	150.00
Car Gasoline/Oil	150.00
Car Maintenance and Repair	181.58
Clothes	200.00
Dry Cleaning	10.00
Charitable	250.00
Entertainment	331.67
Food/Groceries	540.00
Hair	83.33
Legal and Accounting	33.33
Liquor, Beer, Wine	200.00
Pets	166.67
Restaurants	300.00
Sports/Hobbies/Lessons	240.00
Subscriptions, Books	20.00
Toiletries/Grooming/Drug Store	20.00
Vacations	416.67
Health Insurance	813.00
Other Health	143.33
State Taxes	259.00
Capital Expense Provision	500.00
Total Living Expenses	**$6,844.00**

Sally needs $82,000 a year (after tax) to maintain her lifestyle. Can she do it?

- Will she need to downsize?
- Will she need to get a job?
- Will she need to reduce her lifestyle?

Sally wants to know before agreeing to move forward

Then Sally was able to see how much money she could take out of her mutual funds each month and each year. When she saw the return on the mutual funds, she could plan for her annual income and the tax profile she should assume.

Sally's Share of Assets

	Sally Amount	Pct
Real Estate Equity		
Marital Home	$720,000	
Total Value	$720,000	
Equity	$720,000	
Cash & Investments		
T Rowe Price - R	$165,074	
Vanguard - J	$1,000,706	
Fidelity Fund - J	$86,608	
Pax World Fund - J	$49,636	
Pax World Fund - F	$9,987	
Village Bank chk J	$0	
Village Bank - F	$4,133	
Total Investments	$1,316,144	38%
Cars and Personal Effects		
Other Property	$30,000	
Other Property	$0	
Total Personal Items	$30,000	60%
Subtotal Non-Retirement	$2,066,144	49%
IRA/401ks		
Vanguard IRA	$508,770	
Vanguard 403(b)	$2,415	
Vanguard IRA	$5,372	
Total IRA/401ks	$516,557	50%
Subtotal Retirement	$516,557	50%
Total Assets	$2,582,701	49%

- How much can Sally take out every month/year?

- What return should she plan for?

- What tax profile should she assume?

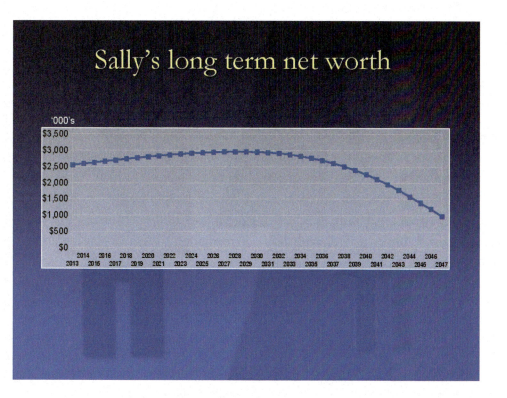

The above graph shows that Sally's assets, if she was living in the marital home, would last until she was ninety-two years of age. Sally said she wasn't likely to live in the home for that long, but this information helped her understand that she could live on her interest and dividends from mutual funds without working very much, or at all, until her advanced years. She was prepared to take the house and land that she and Bill valued at $720,000, along with her portfolio of mutual funds. Financial specialist Chris Chen, from Insight Financial Strategists in Waltham, MA., attended two of our sessions and helped Sally feel secure about her decision to keep the house and, in fact, helped Bill feel secure about purchasing a home about $300,000 below the price of Sally's home in the same community.

This is one of many examples that illustrate how the collaborative mediation approach works (the divorce mediator bringing in the financial specialist is "collaborative mediation"). Other examples include having a financial specialist do a support analysis to arrive at child support or unallocated child support and alimony scenarios, or having the financial specialist help determine the scenario that will leave couples with the most desirable net disposable incomes after taxes. A third example is having the financial specialist value defined benefit pensions and differentiate between cash value defined benefit pensions and those that are not required to be valued. Another benefit of the collaborative mediation process is that qualified domestic relations orders to divide defined benefit pension plans may be drawn to accompany the couples' mediated separation agreement before it goes to their attorneys for review. Couples may use collaborative mediation to resolve pension and detailed support issues, along with health and life insurance, division of assets, and parenting plans, within a single collaborative process.

*Graphs/Charts in this chapter were designed by Chris Chen, CFA, CDFP, Insight Financial Strategists, Waltham, Massachusetts

CHAPTER 12
Mediation versus Negotiation

Seth and Sophie, Anne and Sam, and Ceci and Neil had their decision-making processes mediated through a neutral third party. Laura and Caleb negotiated their conflict about where to go on vacation on their own at home, until they gave up in exasperation and used their mediator to come to a settlement. With their painstaking but successful experience in negotiating where to go on vacation, their next decision-making process should be one they can do on their own. Bill and Sally needed divorce mediation to arrive at the division of their property and to figure out if keeping the marital home was a wise decision.

Many definitions have been offered for *mediation* and *mediator*. My personal favorite definition of a mediator is my own definition, "a neutral professional sitting between two disputing, often 'warring' but 'caring' parties, helping them facilitate resolution, even helping to facilitate healing of their conflicts, problems, and decisions to reach settlements."

My own personal favorite definition of negotiation is "two or more parties meeting to resolve, or even heal their conflicts or problems, or to make decisions, reaching a mutually agreeable solution on their own."

Hopefully, after reaching decisions and resolving conflicts facilitated by a mediator, and with some study of the process, couples or parties will be able to negotiate on their own. The greatest wisdom they can show is to be able to identify the difference between conflicts and decisions, and between those that should be simply negotiated between the parties and those that should be mediated using a competent, neutral professional. Other possible neutrals could be a village elder—a respected member of one's tribe, band, or clan who could be a religious or spiritual leader--- a wise elder in the family, a minister or rabbi, a respected member of the community, or someone who naturally has the skills of a facilitator.

Mediation includes theories, skills, and strategies for negotiation. You saw those theories and skills that I used as I mediated the conflict and decision-making between Anne and Sam and between Seth and Sophie in my office. If the seven steps are the skeleton of the negotiation or mediation process, communication skills used throughout the process are the muscle. As I talk with the parties, without making it too obvious, I try to insert communication suggestions. Here are some examples:

- "Will you state that you *prefer* that she not say that, rather than say, '*Don't you talk to me that way?*' " We need to stay in a 'no-blame frame,' 'a no blame universe' in mediation and negotiation" I often remark.
- Mediator to one or the other party: "Were you feeling very hurt when he proposed this?" *Acknowledgment* comes when someone can say that his or her feelings were very, very hurt. A mediator can state that acknowledging being hurt may be difficult for people who were "shamed" as children. If they said they were sorry, it might mean they would be labeled or seen as being "bad, shameful, inadequate, or inferior" when they may have simply been responding to a younger sibling's provocation. Mediators can say, and individuals can remind themselves, that it is not only okay, but also helpful to say, "I'm sorry," and for the other to say, "I forgive you."
- "Your profound anger is not going to influence the settlement." A mediator may remind people that he or she, as mediator, will not allow the other party to back down in what that person achieves in a settlement when the other person goes into an out-of-control anger.
- A mediator may have to do a lot of work paraphrasing for each person—putting what a party has said in less angry, less toxic tones. Paraphrasing is guesswork, checking out whether his or

her more neutral terms and tones can replace toxic, angry statements. "Correct me if I'm wrong here, Laura. Are you saying that you also want Caleb to get all the rest he needs and that you very much hear him?"
- It is frequently difficult for people to say that they differ with what the other person is saying. Mediators can model less contentious and even gracious ways for people to differ. "Do you think Sam's viewpoint has any merit to it?" "Sounds like Sophie needs a pause in the relationship, and you, Seth, need more intimacy. Those seem like very different needs; neither one is wrong."

Good communication skills and good paraphrasing skills are taught, directly and indirectly, to clients as the mediator uses them while the parties in conflict, or those needing to make a decision, move through the seven-step negotiation and decision-making model. Basic skills in communication need to be followed during the entire mediation or negotiation process. Central to communication skills is doing "active listening," which is:
- not talking or interrupting in any way while the other party is speaking; listening intently, by putting your own thoughts aside to not only *listen* to but also *hear* and *understand* what the other party is really saying and wants you to know. It's being quiet.
- acknowledging what the other person is saying by:
  - nodding your head;
  - saying things like "That's very interesting" or "Can you tell me more about that (now or later)? Obviously you've put a lot of thought into what you're saying."
- summarizing. "You seem to be saying x or y," or "Do I hear that...?" Sift through what the other person has said and glean the most important information, which you then repeat as closely as possible to what you have heard.

- questioning or using open-ended statements. "Are you saying you want to spend a lot more time with your women friends on weekends, Sophie, or that you would actually like to meet new people, including being physical with members of the opposite sex during the separation?"
- explaining to people in conflict that *compromise* is a dirty word in negotiation. We don't want people to meet in the middle, with neither party achieving what he or she wants. We want both parties to be mutually satisfied or at least as mutually satisfied as possible. The middle position will often be a decision that neither party wants nor will enjoy. He may want to see the violent film *Black Mass*, about Whitey Bulger, and she may want to see the light film "Into the Woods." so they settle on seeing a movie neither one wants to see—as a compromise. One couple did this and had to get their money back as coupons to see another movie.

When Seth and Sophie, or other partners, list what matters to them (their "interests" in the Mutual Gains and Getting to Yes models) and their basic human needs, each one should be encouraged to ask the other party clarifying questions so he or she understands the exact meaning of what has been said. In this questioning process, a mediator, or a person-to-person negotiator, can be taught or self-taught to use the above good communication techniques, strategies, and skills. The mediator will use them as a role model of communication that keeps the peace rather than fans the flames.

Good communication skills and good paraphrasing skills are taught, directly and indirectly, to clients. I give this chapter on good communication skills to many couples who are having difficulties staying on track in communicating with one another.

CHAPTER 13
Negotiating the Impossible Vacation Agenda

This is the true story of Madeleine and Adam, a couple in their fifties who successfully negotiated, without the assistance of mediation, a trip to Europe and Eastern Europe in the late spring of 2012.

Adam and Madeleine had been talking about a trip to Cinque Terre, Italy. Cingue Terre is five villages on top of small mountains being connected by walking paths and boats but no roadways. They explored combining that trip with stops in Hallstadt, Vienna, and Salzberg, Austria, where Adam had desired to go for years, and also stays in Croatia on the Adriatic Sea, where the third-cleanest water in the world (after Malta and Cypress) lay offshore and where Madeleine had been dying to go. When they took out a map of Europe and Eastern Europe, they found they had bitten off far more than they could do in one trip. Adam's first priority was visiting Hallstadt, Austria, a tiny, beautiful, six-thousand-year-old town, where salt mining was done in ancient times, located on an unbelievably gorgeous lake. Madeleine's first priority was being by and on the crystalline, turquoise waters of the Adriatic Sea.

Could these two combine their Steps I and II, their wants and bottom-line basic needs, with Step III, what mattered to them most, into the same trip? Surprisingly, using the seven-step model, they did it. They completed the trip, reporting back on how successful the negotiated plan had been and how many times they want to return to nearby places they have yet to see in Croatia and nearby countries.

After college Madeleine had done a lot of traveling alone, using her mother's airline passes until she was twenty-five, as her mother worked for a major airline. She was used to solo travel and loved it as a way to reach out and meet new people. As she and Adam were generating creative options, Madeleine proposed that they didn't have to do the whole trip together. Adam had never traveled alone before and didn't rate that option as high as Madeleine did. She took Adam's word for it that the five lands, isolated but interconnected towns on the northern Italian coast, would be someplace she would like to visit. The pictures of the coastline were impressive. During the brainstorming step, Madeleine suggested that Adam go to Austria alone, where he would be deeply satisfied, especially visiting the beautiful, ancient town of Hallstadt on the lake and Mozart's home in Salzberg, as well as attending classical concerts and opera performances. Madeleine had lived in Germany during her adolescence and had forgotten how to speak German. Since then she had become fluent in Spanish, so she preferred visiting cultures where she could either speak Spanish with the native peoples in their language, or not even expect to be able to. She also wasn't at all fond of sauerkraut and didn't fashion gaining weight on the pastries she knew she would not be able to resist. She assumed Austria was a lot like Germany but wasn't sure.

Thinking about how much she did not want to go to Austria, except for Hallstadt, Madeleine put on the option list that she go to the five lands on the Italian coast with Adam. Still another of Madeleine's options was that she head to the eastern Italian coast from Cinque Terre to catch some kind of boat to the Croatian coast (the "new Riviera"), which she was absolutely dying to visit. Adam expressed wonderment that Madeleine would want to leave her plans so open. He said that if he were going to Austria alone, he would get his train ticket on the Internet, with the hours and track numbers to Austria from Italy before leaving the United States. "How could Madeleine leave things so loose?" Adam pondered to himself and then to Madeleine. She expressed that as an adventure traveler she preferred being able to make up her mind at the last minute, going south instead of west depending on her interest and the weather. They began to see that they could take a trip together if it didn't have to be together for the entire trip. He needed security, and she needed spontaneity, their different bottom-line human needs.

Adam was eager to add to the options list that he join Madeleine in Split, Croatia, after his trip to Austria. The two made supposals and proposals and reached mutual agreement that they would go to Cinque Terre, Italy, together; Adam would go to Hallstadt, Vienna, and Salzberg, Austria, by train; Madeleine would travel to Venice and then find a boat to Croatia, where the two would meet. When they reported back, Madeleine was utterly delighted to say that her sense of adventure and leaving things loose had resulted in a last-minute Mediterranean cruise from Venice on the Costa Fascinosa, the replacement ship for the Costa Constancia that went down the previous season when it hit a reef off the coast of Giglia, an island west of Italy. She called the ship line on the Monday she arrived in Venice, which was dreary and rainy, determined to get on a ship as soon as possible. At first she was told there was no passage and then that there was a large room for a disabled person available that afternoon for a discount. Madeleine was good to go! By 3:00 p.m. she was on the Costa Fascinosa, ready to set sail.

The ship stopped in Bari, in southern Italy, and at Olympia, Rhodes, and Santorini in the Greek Islands, allowing her an early departure in Dubrovnik, Croatia. She and Adam met up in Split, Croatia, where they explored Roman ruins and relaxed on Hvar, that gorgeous island and an archipelago, off the coast. The two proceeded to Dubrovnik, which they found delightful, and Madeleine went south to Montenegro to sail the Bay of Kotor after Adam had to leave for work at home.

Adam had savored the music and culture of Austria, including the precious, ancient lakeside town of Hallstadt, and Madeleine had dipped into the Adriatic Sea from the shores of precious Croatian islands and explored the intrigues of Montenegro, a country north of Albania that she hadn't even heard of before this trip. The two of them were deeply satisfied with the conjoint trip, which would have ended badly if either of them had had to sacrifice what mattered most to him or her. Adam made a separate photograph album of his Austrian trip, and Madeleine's photograph album included many islands off the coast of Croatia. They had done well with their own negotiation.

Definition of the Issue

It's January. We want to take a trip to Cinque Terre, Italy; Croatia; and Austria this summer. One person wants to take in Hallstadt, Austria, and the cultural events in Salzberg and Vienna, Austria. The other wants to be in Croatia, by, on, and in the water, and wants to explore ancient Roman ruins.

Step I: "I Want" Positions

I want:
Madeleine

- "I want to go to Europe and Eastern Europe this summer."

I want:
Adam

- "I want to go to Cinque Terre, Italy, and Austria this summer."

Step II: My Bottom-Line Need

Madeleine

- Spontaneous adventure. Not to be hampered by too much planning.

Adam

- Security. To have bought every ticket and know every track I'll be on in Europe.

Step III: What *Really, Really* Matters to Me

Madeline:	Rate 1-5	Adam:	Rate 1-5
"We go to Cinque Terre, Italy together."	5	"We go to Cinque Terre together."	5
"You go to Hallstadt, Vienna, and Salzberg yourself. I want to sail from Venice to Dubrovnik, Croatia, by boat."	5	"We go to Hallstadt, Austria together."	5
"I will have an Adriatic-Aegean ocean passage by myself and I want to swim in the crystalline waters off the coast of Croatia."	5	"I vote 'two' that Madeline has an Adriatic-Aegean ocean passage by herself."	2
"I go to the country of Montenegro, south of Croatia, when you have to get back to work, Adam. And I sail on the Bay of Kotor."	5	"I wish I could go to the islands off Croatia. I give you a 'five' for going on your own, since I'll be in Austria."	5
"Not being held to a timeline by too much advance planning."	5	"Oh, no, I wish I could go to Montenegro and the Bay of Kotor, too, but I do have to get back to work."	5
		"Having tickets in advance of leaving the country to have a sense of security."	5

Step IV: Best Personal Alternative

Madeleine said later that her personal best alternative would have been to take her trip to Croatia and Montenegro for the entire time, not bothering to go to Italy. Adam said he very much wanted to do the whole trip with Madeleine but would have given up Cinque Terre, Italy, and gone to Austria and met Madeleine in Croatia.

Step V: Brainstorming

BRAINSTORMING CREATIVE OPTIONS and IDEAS	Madeline	Adam
Adam and Madeleine: "We go to Cinque Terre, Italy, together."	5	5
Adam: "We go to Hallstadt, Austria, together."	1	5
Adam:" I go to Austria–to Hallstadt, Vienna and Salzberg."	5	5
Madeleine: "I have an Adriatric–Aegean Ocean passage to Dubrovnik."	5	2
Madeleine: "I go to islands off from Dubrovnik before Adam arrives from Austria."	5	3
Madeleine: "I go to the southern country of Montenegro by myself after Adam has to leave to come home to work."	5	3

Step VI: Agreement Building—Supposals and Proposals

Adam and Madeleine paid close attention to what *really, really* mattered to one another. Although Adam had never traveled alone, he wanted to go to Austria so much that this became an option for him.

Adam's initial supposal was "I go to Hallstadt, Vienna, and Salzberg, Austria, by myself, buying tickets online before we leave." Madeleine agreed with this and counter-supposed that both of them go to Cinque Terre, Italy, and then she would travel by train to Venice, where she hoped to catch ocean passage to Croatia. Adam reluctantly agreed to that, as he wanted Madeleine to come to Austria with him. She said she would wait for Adam in Split, Croatia, where he would fly in by plane.

Those were their agreements before leaving this country. Who would have known that Madeleine, who liked adventure and leaving plans loose, would find passage on a cruise ship for the day after she arrived in Venice? As cited before, the beautiful cruise ship stopped in Bari, Italy, and Olympia, Santorini, and Rhodes, Greece, with stops at all ports for tours, before allowing Madeleine to disembark early in Dubrovnik, Croatia rather than going on to the last stop in Venice. After arriving in Dubrovnik, Madeleine visited many islands off the coast of Dubrovnik and two off the coast of Split, Croatia, before greeting Adam who was coming from Austria where he had toured to his heart's content. He was so excited he could barely speak. Upon arrival home, Adam constructed his own photograph album of Austria which he showed off to all his friends, while Madeleine constructed a separate album of the turquoise islands of Croatia and of Montenegro, where she had sailed around Kotor Bay eating sausages and cheese, dancing and drinking wine with Bosnians, Serbians and Croatians aboard. The couple was aglow with how satisfactory their trip had been.

Step VII: A Mutual Agreement

Adam and Madeleine will go to Cinque Terre, Italy, together. Adam will carefully plan his trip to Hallstadt, Salzberg, and Vienna, Austria. Madeleine will go to Venice and via boat to Dubrovnik, Croatia, and meet Adam in Split, Croatia, from where they will go to Hvar, Croatia, and a beautiful archipelago. Both will go back to Dubrovnik, and Madeleine will travel to Montenegro.

Peace Begins with Us

CHAPTER 14
Baseball or Violin for Marco?

Luiz and Kyoko seemed like the quintessential odd couple: she demure, Japanese, shaping her hands into a temple position, and bowing before she spoke; and he, much grittier, a no-holds-barred, pull-no-punches type. How on earth did they get together? As a minor league baseball player, Luiz had been introduced to Kyoko by her brother, who was Luiz's teammate. They fell in love and respected the high level of competence each displayed in their work—he in baseball, she in music.

When a tiny baseball bat was placed on their son Marco's tummy shortly after his birth, Kyoko never gave it another thought. She knew citizens of the Dominican Republic wanted their baby boys to play baseball and bring financial fortunes to their families. It was symbolic, only a gesture, she thought.

Marco was now 3½ and Kyoko was about to sign him up for Suzuki violin lessons. After all, she was a concert violinist, and her mother and grandmother played stringed instruments as well. To hear her representation, this talent went back to the original Japanese dynasty! The couple had found their way to mediation through friends who had been privy to the sparks flying, even though Kyoko's ethos was never to display conflict, especially outside the family. It was quite a stretch for her to come to mediation.

Luiz had begun to pitch to Marco and had him catching but not yet running bases. He wanted to start recruiting Marco's small friends for serious instruction during the summer in their big backyard and secretly thought that violin lessons were "sissy stuff." Besides, Luiz wanted to see if their son had talent and could follow in his footsteps. Maybe he could even get into the major leagues. There wouldn't be time in a busy, suburban family's schedule for Suzuki lessons, he was certain, so he asked Kyoko to hold off on the lessons until he could determine whether their son liked baseball and had any talent. Luiz and Kyoko dug in their heels. Neither of them could stand in the other's shoes to see how important it was to each of them to pass on their individual legacy to Marco. Luiz and Kyoko strongly felt that neither they nor Marco could put in the time for him to be fully accomplished in both violin and baseball.

In the office, they presented a portrait of diversity and contrasts. Luiz was large, Kyoko tiny; she was soft-spoken, he spoke loudly and interrupted her comments. The basic ground rules of mediation and negotiation—whether negotiating with or without a mediator—needed to be spelled out:

- One speaker should not interrupt or talk over the other speaker. The negotiators should be continually reminded if they don't at first observe this ground rule.
- The volume of an angry voice will not influence the outcome of the negotiation.
- Initially they were asked to communicate through the mediator and not to yell at one another.
- They were asked to be seated so they could look into each other's eyes and remain doing so.
- They were reminded that loving touches are helpful to intimate partners. (For business partners, a firm handshake works better!)

Kyoko explained, of course, that she *wanted* (Step I) Marco to start with Suzuki lessons as soon as possible, while Luiz *wanted* (Step I) their son to get as much practice with baseball as possible. Kyoko *needed* (Step II) recognition that her family's instrumental talents had gone back centuries and should continue. Luiz also *needed* (Step II) recognition that he, alone, had changed his family's well-being financially and in terms of reputation and he wanted his son to continue his legacy.

What *really, really* mattered (Step III) to Kyoko was that Marco have the opportunity to begin Suzuki to see if he liked playing and if he had talent. What *really, really* mattered to Luiz (Step III) was that Marco not just begin playing baseball but also that he achieve at least the rank Luiz had achieved—and perhaps go even further than he had to the major leagues.

Neither Kyoko nor Luiz shared their Step IV: Best Personal Alternative with one another, most likely in this case because they were, well, frankly, sneaky. We later learned that if she couldn't negotiate a deal with Luiz, Kyoko had in mind signing Marco up for a short series of violin lessons without saying anything. Luiz had in mind doing some backyard training with Marco and some other kids at a teammate's house when Kyoko was at work. Luckily, after Kyoko had Marco do some under-the-table preliminary lessons in violin, and Luiz had rehearsed baseball with Marco behind Kyoko's back, they didn't have to employ what looked like WPAs (worst possible alternatives) instead of BPAs (best possible alternatives) as they were able to negotiate a mutual agreement.

Step I: "I Want" Positions

I want:
Kyoko

I want:
Luiz

- "Marco to begin Suzuki lessons as soon as time permits"
- "Marco to begin baseball lessons as soon as weather permits"

Step II: My Bottom-Line Need

Kyoto

- for my family's legacy as stringed instrumentalists to be carried on and recognized by Luiz
- to see if Marco has talent with the violin

Luiz

- to see if Marco has the talent to earn fame and fortune in baseball
- to receive recognition that he, Luiz, had changed the financial circumstances of his family and brought them recognition

Step III: What *Really, Really* Matters to Me

Kyoto

- That Marco have the opportunity to begin playing the violin and see if he has talent

Luiz

- That Marco begin playing baseball with the aim of achieving at least minor league status

Step IV: Best Personal Alternative

Both Kyoko and Luiz acted in underhanded ways in determining what could be done if they couldn't negotiate a settlement with the other person. Kyoko took Marco to a series of preliminary violin lessons, in which she determined that he not only had aptitude but also enjoyed playing the violin very much. Luiz played baseball with Marco and some of his friends outside in the cold, while the ground was still hard, and determined that Marco had great hand-eye coordination, could pitch well, bat hard, and liked the sport.

Step V: Brainstorming

	BRAINSTORMING CREATIVE OPTIONS and IDEAS	Kyoto	Luiz
1.	Kyoko: "Let's enter Marco in Suzuki for a semester, see how he does and how he likes it, and then think about baseball after that."	5	1
2.	Luiz: "Let me form a kids baseball team first, see how he does and how he likes it, before we think about expensive musical lessons."	1	5
3.	Kyoko: "Why don't you just practice in the yard with Marco, see how he does, and evaluate?"	5	1
4.	Luiz: "Well, Kyoko, why don't *you* just practice at home with Marco on a rented violin, and we'll see how he does, while I form a serious little team with him in the backyard?"	1	5
5.	Kyoko: "Let's enter Marco in both activities for the summer and then have Janet speak with Marco about how much he likes both activities."	4	4

These two parents could not generate any more options. None. There were no options close to one another, and none to eliminate. There was nothing left to do but start to generate supposals and proposals. How far would we get with this endeavor?

Step VI: Agreement Building—Supposals and Proposals

- Luiz suggested, i.e., supposed, that they would *never* come to agreement.
- Kyoko agreed. "There is no middle ground here."
- Kyoko proposed that even though time was limited for Marco to undertake both activities at the same time, they could each take responsibility for enrolling him in or teaching him the activity of their choice for the upcoming summer. It was the only

way things would work. Then, when the summer Suzuki program ends, Marco will have attended enough baseball and violin practices to evaluate his talent and have a neutral third party, Janet, talk with Marco about what he felt and thought his short- and long-term preferences might be in each of these fields.

- Luiz proposed that they try very hard to *not* put Marco in the middle, trying to persuade him to like Luiz's or Kyoko's family legacy the best. He suggested that they just listen to Marco, hear him out, and observe to what level, if any, he wanted to engage in each activity.

Kyoko couldn't believe her ears. Her husband was much more sensitive to Marco's needs than she had perceived up to this time. He had been hanging out with her very sensible brother, and she believed some good sense had rubbed off on her husband.

Step VII: A Mutual Agreement

Luiz and Kyoko decided that each of them would introduce Marco to their activity of choice during the summer, listening to him and observing his preferences for the amount of time he devoted to each activity. In addition, they would have a neutral evaluator speak with Marco about his summer experiences. "After all, heaven help us, he might want to and have talent to continue in both activities," said Luiz.

Peace Begins with Us

CHAPTER 15
The Seven Visual Steps: Skeleton and Muscle

In decision-making mediation, couples are encouraged to choose the number of sessions they believe they will need to get to resolution. It is often six to eight 1½- or two-hour sessions or twelve one-hour sessions. People do make decisions, of course, in a single or several sessions. If they haven't reached resolution in the number of sessions they have chosen, we carve out another series of sessions. If they reach resolution before the stated number of carved-out sessions, they are finished, with their decision, solution, or settlement made. They might choose to undergo another series of sessions to implement their decisions. For example, if they've decided to reconcile and work on their marriage, they may do reconciliation therapy or couples mediation. If they've decided to separate or divorce, they may decide to undertake separation or divorce mediation. More and more time is not on our side. James Mann in *Time-Limited Psychotherapy* convinced me not to prolong interventions.

I suggest that if you do a negotiation on your own, follow this same prescription, identifying in advance how many sessions of negotiation you believe you will need to reach resolution. Setting the stage for your in-person negotiations, with or without a mediator, is vital. Each person needs to give his or her version of the definition of the issue, problem, negotiation, or decision they are confronting. You won't usually have the same definition or perspective. We attempt, however, to reach agreement on the mutual definition of the issue. Reaching as close to the same definition of the issue is important.

As you are beginning your negotiation, review the Seven Visual Steps to Yes:
- Step I: Our "I want" positions
- Step II: Our individual basic, bottom-line human needs

- Step III: What *really, really* matters to each of us relative to the conflict
- Step IV: Our individual best personal alternatives
- Step V: Brainstorming: Generating Options and Ideas for Agreement
- Step VI: Our supposals and proposals to build agreement
- Step VII: Our mutual agreement

These steps are the skeleton of the Seven Visual Steps to Yes and are listed in Index I.

Everyone in the negotiation or mediation should have a printed copy of the steps. The muscles are the communication methods and strategies, which everyone should learn before undertaking the seven steps. These methods are listed in chapter 15 and may be copied and distributed to clients.

Here are more communication methods and strategies:

A. Staging the Negotiation

- Find a quiet, undisturbed location.
- Sit where people can look each other in the eyes
- Sit close enough but not too close
- Remind each other that the issue or problem is what they need to focus on, and that the other person is not the adversary or the problem
- Ask each other if they have the motivation and capacity to work on the negotiation at that time. If not, postpone work on the negotiation to a better time.
- Make a *decision* to talk quietly and to be classy and sophisticated in your communications, not to be defensive, and not to label, devalue, or undermine the other party. If you are interrupting one another, *stop it and start again*!
- Make a decision to allow the humble and confident presentations of yourself to combine.

B. Active Listening

- Be quiet while the other person is speaking. Don't interrupt him or her.
- Listen intently, putting aside your own thoughts to understand what he or she is actually telling you. If you can't do this, practice using a watch and talk to each other for a designated amount of time, say five minutes.
- Acknowledge what the other is saying by:
  - nodding your head,
  - saying things like "That's interesting" or "I hadn't thought of that" or "Tell me more about that (now or later),"
  - letting the other person know you value him or her.
- Summarize: "You're saying…is that correct?" Sift through what one has said, gleaning the most important information, which you repeat to the other person.
- Ask questions and more questions:
  - "Are you saying…suggesting?"
  - "Could you say that in a different way?"
  - "What is the most important thing to you that you've said?"
- Restate: Change negative statements into positive statements and change "you" statements to "I" statements: For example, "I feel deflated" rather than "You *are a real drag* on my self-esteem" or " I hear that you've put a lot of thought into this" rather than "You're just talking ragtime."
- Learn to paraphrase, taking the angry toxins out of what is being said:
  - Instead of saying, "You're saying that I've never spent two days in a row with those kids," say, "You're saying that you think you understand my need for exactly the same amount of time with the children that you have, but your impression is that this won't provide enough consistency and predictability for the kids during the school week. Is that what you're saying?"

- Instead of saying, "I am *not* going to *not* live with my children under any circumstances," say, "I'm saying that my heart is breaking when I think about not being with our kids every morning when they get up!"

C. Apology

Learn the art of apology, saying "I'm sorry" with sincerity, remorse, and forgiveness, and the other person replying with a sincere "I do forgive you."

D. Correct Thinking

Learn to correct errors in thinking.

"All or none" and "either/or" thinking: "My adopted daughter can't have ADHD; we were told she had fetal alcohol syndrome." "If I'm right, you're wrong", rather than more correctly stating "We both have our own perspectives and they differ."

Right from the beginning of negotiation or decision-making, the mediator will talk with each client on the telephone for introductions, goal setting, symmetry, and neutrality, and of course, as stated before, each client will be urged to come in with his or her definition of the issue to be negotiated, the problem to be solved, or the decision to be made. In other words, each person will state his or her goal, and the two negotiators will find a way to combine the goals into a single definition of what will be negotiated.

When negotiating between two or more parties, the ground rules are to allow the other person to speak, trying to keep the amount of communication equal between them. The stage for the negotiation should be set when both people have a relatively tranquil physical environment and a fairly tranquil internal environment—not during times when their children need them or when one or the other is highly upset after an argument.

When you or your negotiating partner have reached a boiling point, ask your partner if he or she would mind if you take a five-minute or longer break to compose yourself, cool down, and chill out. Reenter the discussion or negotiation less stressed and maybe with a smile.

To do the seven-step negotiation, both people need to acquaint themselves with good communication skills, practicing them in a number of different environments before undertaking the negotiation. Then, if the steps get derailed, you will know how to calmly address the emotional issues before moving on with the steps. Either person may be of tremendous value to the other when he or she has lost his or her cool, remembering good negotiation skills and placing them on the table. Remember that you are on the same side of that negotiating table, together, with the issue being addressed on the other side of the table. Before beginning a mediated Seven Visual Steps to Yes process or one done on your own, all parties may want to review Index I, the Seven Visual Steps to Yes, and this chapter on communication skills and strategies. Mediators may review Index II, Mediation Strategies.

CHAPTER 16
Can We Afford a Garage and a Vacation?

The last conflict we are going to illustrate is between Melissa and Gregg who made a decision while in mediation about their twins' behavior and designing consequences for it. They went even furrther to decide if they could afford to build a garage and take a two-week vacation.

Definition of the Conflict
"After the record snowstorm of 2015, can we afford to build a garage this summer and take a two-week vacation?"

It was the late spring after the great snowfall of 2015 when snows drifted eight to ten feet in the northeastern United States. Melissa was itching to take a family vacation, and Gregg knew he had to build a two-car garage to keep the snows off their cars next winter. Without being able to go outside, Melissa had become considerably depressed from March to June 2015 and absolutely knew she had to have a vacation. Gregg had thrown his back out getting on top of the cars to scrape off the snow and absolutely knew they had to have a garage to keep the cars clean next winter.

Gregg and Melissa had two middle-school-aged twins whose comportment and the consequences for it they were already discussing in family mediation. The twins were begging for a summer vacation. The defined conflict between the couple was "Can we afford to build the new garage this summer and take a vacation as well? We need to make a decision."

Step I: "I Want" Positions

This might also be asked as "What would you feel so good about achieving here?" or "What are you dying to achieve here?" (This step is called "positions" in the Mutual Gains and Getting to Yes models.)

I WANT X!	WELL, I WANT Y!
Melissa	Gregg

- "I want to take a long, restful vacation."
- "I want to build a garage."

Step II: My Bottom-Line Need

This step was adapted from Abraham Maslow's *Hierarchy of Human Needs* and Herb Kelman and John Bolton's *Basic Human Needs*.

Examples again are:

- A sense of fairness
- A sense of home
- Financial security
- A sense of emotional security for me and/or for me with the children
- A sense of safety
- Feeling respected
- Feeling recognized
- A sense of freedom
- A sense of autonomy
- Confidence in who I am/in my identity
- A sense of belongingness
- A sense of love
- Relaxation
- Something else

If a mediator is mediating the negotiation and a party can't come up with a bottom-line need, the mediaor can prompt the party by giving him or her a copy of the above list.

Melissa	**Gregg**
• I *need* time off from work.	• I *need* to have the cars in a garage this winter so I don't have to shovel or blow snow.
• I *need* time together with the family.	

Step III: What *Really, Really* Matters to Me

Melissa:	Rate:	Gregg:	Rate:
"We haven't had a restful vacation as a family in four years."	5	"We haven't had a restful vacation as a family in four years"	5
"Time together as a family for bonding is necessary before the older kids don't want to vacation with us anymore."	5	"Time together as a family for bonding is necessary before the older kids go to college. We're still three years away from that."	5
"I hear you about the garage, the snowplowing and shoveling, and your back, but we could hire a service to plow us out. I think the vacation is more important than the garage. I was profoundly depressed this last winter."	5	"Last winter with drifted snows piled up eight to ten feet, I practically broke my back snow-blowing and shoveling. I need a garage and a plowing service costs fifty dollars for big snows."	5
"I'm willing to compromise and camp part of the vacation or go to our low-cost hotel in Wellfleet."	5	"First we have to deal with building the garage before the onslaught of the winter; don't even think of camping or the hotel."	5

Step IV: Best Personal Alternative

Melissa knew that her best personal alternative was to take the weekdays with her children at the campsite, or with her children and friends, and beg Gregg to come to the Cape for each or part of each weekend at their reasonably priced hotel. Gregg knew that he had the same best personal alternative as Melissa.

Step V: Brainstorming

	BRAINSTORMING CREATIVE OPTIONS and IDEAS	Melissa	Gregg
1.	Melissa: "I go with Ellen and their children to the Audubon Campground, for a week, and you and Mark come that weekend and the next week we will all go to the Wellfleet Hotel."	5	5
2.	Gregg: "I work on framing the garage while you are gone to Cape Cod for two weeks."	5	5
3.	Gregg: "Suppose we build the garage this summer and take a vacation next summer?"	1	5
4.	Melissa: "Let's get your brothers to help us build the garage for a big discount and go to the Cape as well to vacation together as a family."	5	1
5.	Gregg: "Whether it's just you and I and our kids or whether Ellen and Mark can join us, we need to go when the rates are lower after Labor Day."	5	5
6.	Melissa: "We rent a house for two weeks on the Cape with Ellen and Mark, and you and Mark come down for long weekends and whenever you can during the week."	5	4

Step VI: Agreement Building—Supposals and Proposals

- Melissa and Gregg were ready to use supposals and proposals. This step is a bridge from brainstorming creative ideas and options to arriving at a mutual agreement. It starts out tentatively with supposals (suppose we "x or y") and moves on to the making of offers in the form of proposals. This example began with the wife wanting to take a summer vacation and the husband wanting to build a garage. Gregg (supposal): "*Suppose* we build the new garage this summer and take a vacation next summer?"
- Melissa: (counter-supposal): "*Suppose* we take two weeks at Cape Cod this summer and build the garage as well? We need a family vacation."
- Gregg (second counter-supposal): "Still too expensive. Suppose you camp at the campgrounds, I come down as much as I can, and we build the garage?"
- Melissa (proposal): "I propose we rent a house with Ellen, Mark, and their children while you work on the garage, and you come down for long weekends and whenever you can. We need a rest and some family time together."
- Gregg (counter-proposal): "All right to the above, as long as we wait to build the garage until after Labor Day when the hotel rental rates are lower, and then I can come down two weekends."
- Melissa agrees with Gregg's counter-proposal, which becomes Step VII.

Step VII: A Mutual Agreement

We agree to build the new garage this summer. We agree that we rent a house with Ellen, Mark, and their children for the first two weeks after Labor Day and that Gregg and Mark come down two long weekends or at least two weekends or whenever possible.

Peace Begins with Us

CHAPTER 17
The Importance of Being Earnest When Using the 1–5 Rating Systems

You may remember that a member of the Rhode Island Divorce Mediators Association and someone in the Massachusetts Council on Family Mediation said that she thought the rating system for Step III: What *Really, Really* Matters to Me and Step V: Brainstorming was the most important part of the Seven Visual Steps to Yes. When people see in black and *fright* how they have rated their priorities for what *really, really* matters to them and to which options and ideas they have given four and five ratings, they may begin to create packages of supposals and proposals that could lead to Step VII: A Mutual Agreement. *The numbers don't lie;* they can't be disputed. These are what *matter* to each person, their top priorities and highest-rated options and ideas. The ratings are a simple but unbelievably direct manner of getting at what two people, together know to be their highest truth.

CHAPTER 18
Origins of the Seven Visual Steps to Yes

Seven Visual Steps to Yes Is Built Upon the Other Major Negotiation Approaches

The Seven Visual Steps to Yes did not spring forth full blown as my creation of course. Howard Raiffa, the MIT professor, wrote *The Art and Science of Negotiation*; Lawrence Susskind, in collaboration with Roger Fisher, William Ury, and the original founders of the Program on Negotiation, invented the Mutual Gains Approach at MIT; and Roger Fisher and William Ury produced "principled negotiation" or the Getting to Yes approach at Harvard University.

The Mutual Gains negotiation project originated with scholars and practitioners at the Consensus Building Institute, a Cambridge, Massachusetts,-based company founded by Susskind. The four steps of this approach are (1) prepare, (2) explore interests on both sides, and create value 3) distribute value, and (4) follow through. These are taken from Susskind's "Arguing, Bargaining, and Getting Agreement" article in *The Oxford Handbook of Public Policy*. Here are the four steps or stages:

PREPARE	EXPLORE INTERESTS	DISTRIBUTE VALUE	FOLLOW THROUGH
Clarify your mandate and define your team	Explore interests on both sides	Behave in ways that build trust	Agree on monitoring arrangements
Estimate your Best Alternative to Negotiated Agreement (BATNA) and theirs	Suspend criticism	Discuss standards or criteria for "dividing" the pie	Make it easy to live up to commitments
Improve your BATNA (if possible)	Invent without committing	Use neutrals to suggest possible distributions	Align organizational incentives and controls
Think about their interests	Generate options and packages that "make the pie larger"	Design nearly self-enforcing agreements	Keep working to improve relationships
			Agree to use neutrals to resolve disagreements

In contrast to these lengthy four steps of the Mutual Gains Approach, the Seven Visual Steps to Yes are visual,—with faces and boxes-; they're colloquial, compact, visual, with examples, which enable the users to bring them to mind quickly when they have important decisions to make and important conflicts to resolve. "What did Anne and Sam do? What did Bill and Sally do?"

The Mutual Gains Approach is the Holy Grail from which the Seven Visual Steps to Yes evolved. It initially mentions knowing one's own and the other party's interests. I mention knowing what "*really, really* matters" in Step III of the Seven Visual Steps to Yes, which is virtually the same thing.

Our Step V: Brainstorming is a core concept in negotiation and decision-making. Stage two (Create Value) in the Mutual Gains Approach— "generates options and *package*s that make the pie larger"—is more explicit than our Step V. Keep in mind that our "supposals and proposals" often build packages by combining ideas: one or more supposals are often offered with a proposal or proposals to the negotiation partner as a package.

The second stage of Mutual Gains "invents ideas without committing" while the Seven Visual Steps does this in Step VI: Agreement Building, which also creates or invents ideas without committing.

I added "What is your basic human need?" but that is left out of the Mutual Gains Approach, and the principles of the Getting to Yes approach, the former which is lengthy, nonvisual, and without case studies, more difficult to remember than the Seven Visual Steps to Yes.

The Mutual Gains Approach goes further than the Seven Visual Steps to Yes in "discovering standards or criteria for expanding the pie." Expanding the pie is something that Adnan and Sherrie did in building a workshop for Adnan in their basement. Mutual Gains talks about "making it easy to live up to commitments," something we should help decision-makers with when they reach our Step VII: A Mutual Agreement. Mutual Gains adds "behave in ways that build trust" and "suspend criticism." We can mention that to every couple mediating an agreement.

In the sixth step (Agreement Building—Supposals and Proposals) of the Seven Visual Steps to Yes, two or more parties will initiate and then offer alternatives that will lead to a "fair agreement." They will feel within themselves that they each have received a "fair share" in the agreement. In Step V, it is made clear that the generation of ideas and options can easily be combined to reach a win-win solution or mutual agreement.

The Seven Visual Steps to Yes model incorporates much of the Mutual Gains Approach, but our steps are compactly and visually packaged with faces and informational boxes. The seven-step method reaches out and visually grabs the participants reading about the conflict to be resolved or the decision to be made and gives them case studies of the Seven Visual Steps to Yes. The reader can remember the steps of a particular conflict mentioned in the book and remember specific cases later when they are on the verge of a difficult argument or conflict. They can see those faces, those wants and needs, what really matters to them, their best alternatives, their brainstormed options, their supposals and proposals, and their mutual agreements right in front of their eyes and reproduce them in their own decision-making or conflict resolution.

The four principles of negotiation highlighted in the Getting to Yes approach, the other gold standard of negotiation, are:
1. Separate the people from the problem.
2. Focus on interests not positions.
3. Invent options for mutual gain.
4. Insist on using objective criteria.

The first two principles are not built into Seven Visual Steps to Yes, although they are good, even necessary principles. Let's keep them in mind in every conflict, problem, or issue we resolve or decision we make. Laura and Caleb were initially tempted to make each other the problem or the adversary before they settled into keeping the problem in front of them on the other side of the table. They were tempted to not separate the people from the problem.

In *Getting to Yes*, Fisher and Ury also speak about "basic human needs," derived from Abraham Maslow and borrowed by Herbert Kelman at Harvard's Weatherhead Project and John Bolton, the Australian scholar and diplomat who taught at Colorado University. They don't give basic needs the central emphasis I give them in Step II: My Bottom-Line Need," relating to the decision, negotiation, conflict, or issue. This helps people get to fundamental or foundational aspects of what they want and need.

In addition to being more colloquial and visual (pictures are worth a thousand words), the Seven Visual Steps to Yes is different from the two approaches in these ways:

1. I believe people can understand the question "What do you *want?*" much more easily than "What is your position?" Not only could *position* mean "my opinion," but it could also refer to my type of employment, where I've been placed, my rank in society, the way I hold my violin, and so on. Asking "What do you *want* in this negotiation?" is infinitely clearer than "What is your position?"
2. What I "bottom-line need" in Step II in the Seven Visual Steps. This is different from what I *want*, or desire. It is something more non-negotiable. I really *need* this in the negotiation. This is a new and different step than in the other approaches.
3. What "*really, really* matters" to me in the seven-steps method is comparable to "interests" in the two other negotiation approaches cited. But *interest* can mean what I earn on my money in the bank or in the stock market. It can mean my right to claim a certain interest, or percentage, of something. Something can be in my interest or to my advantage. So let's stick with "what *really, really* matters" as our third step. It is much easier to understand than "interests."
4. Step IV: Best Personal Alternative has been much more easily understood than the term BATNA (Best Alternative to a Negotiated Agreement), which has baffled people since its inception. Best personal alternative means if I can't negotiate a deal with the other party to the conflict, issue, or problem, what can I do on my own to gain what it is that I want?
5. Step V: Brainstorming, the generation of creative options and ideas for settlement, carefully considers and includes what really, really matters to the other person. Step III is, of course, the same as "inventing options for mutual gain" in "principled negotiation," or the Mutual Gains Approach.
6. I find the building in of a Step VI in our negotiation approach, "Agreement Building," helps to create a bridge from the generating of creative options, which have been carefully rated,

to a mutual agreement. Partners have eliminated some low-rated creative options and cited the options rated four or five on which they have the most consensus. These options give people the opportunity to try out their tentative "supposals"; have the other party delete, add, or modify them; reach proposals or offers they both can own; and then move on to mutual agreement. Supposals, a prelude to proposals, are softer, gentler, and less threatening to the other partner. "Hey, honey, suppose we build our new garage this summer?" gives the other partner an opportunity *not* to be defensive in reacting to a definite proposal such as "I *propose* we build our garage by the end of the summer!" Partners package their options into supposals and proposals that will end up being their Step VII: A Mutual Agreement. Agreement building is not a step in the other negotiation approaches.

7. There is nothing different in Step VII: Mutual Agreement from saying a "joint solution for mutual gain" or "win-win solution" I simply believe it is easier for people to understand.
8. The rating system of "What *Really, Really* Matters to Me" and "Brainstorming" is fundamental to our Seven Visual Steps to Yes approach. Never forget to rate the ideas that are in the blue and orange boxes. The rating system is not present in the Mutual Gains Approach, the Getting to Yes approach, or *The Art and Science of Negotiation*. Arguably it is the most important part of the Seven Visual Steps to Yes.

You may use this seven-step visual approach in your marriage or personal relationship, with your children, your parents, your relatives, business partners and employees, your friends, or with any other human being. Both of you may be equally acquainted with the process, but you may also use it with another or others who haven't learned it as yet. One spectacular way of using and teaching the process is to have a facilitator, perhaps a psychologist, social worker or religious education teacher, present my PowerPoint slides of Seven Visual Steps to Yes to six or eight pairs of people in your book group, legal group, mediation group, church group, or temple group. Then each member of the group can read this book individually or with his or her partner. Following that, they would come to three or more group sessions, perhaps with the person with whom they need to make a decision, solve a problem, or resolve a conflict. The members of the group will attempt to assist people or partners in making those difficult decisions or resolving difficult conflicts. The group is extended if all eight or so members haven't finished making their decisions or resolving their conflicts or will be made shorter if all pairs have resolved their conflicts or made their decisions. You may use the process with a professional mediator or a neutral colleague or friend. Whenever and however you use it, if you are not afraid to remove familiar patterns and conflicts from your life, you will settle conflicts and make decisions. If you can stand change, use the process; teach it to bring about more and more peace in your own environment. Others will witness your abilities and your changes. They will want to know how you did it.

Afterword

Since time immemorial, humans have been using negotiation. A Neanderthal man, two hundred thousand years ago in Europe, negotiated with another to borrow a tool for the afternoon. Or an Ice Age man may have used a mediator to intercede when he wanted to borrow a spear point from his neighbor. The Greeks, Plato's *The Republic: Book IV*, and the Romans referred to a mediator as internuncio, medium, intercessor, philantropus, interpolator, conciliator, interlocutor, and intrepres (Roman law in 530–533). Elders and wise men in indigenous tribes are reported to have played and continue to play the role of go-betweens.

Teddy Roosevelt played this role; so did Jimmy Carter.

Pope Francis recently intervened to help the United States reach out to Cuba and open diplomatic relations with that country.

The Department of Labor in 1913 rejected arbitration in favor of mediation for their collective bargaining disputes, and the US Congress passed a series of acts dealing with railroad disputes, which was extended to deal with the airline industry.

At the end of the 1970s and into the early 1980s, social workers and family lawyers began training to become (family and divorce) mediators to bring about a paradigm shift, from couples needing to "lawyer up" for divorce litigation, spending excessive amounts of money and time, and exaggerating their conflicts, to giving them the option of having a mediator work amiably with them to bring resolution about parenting plans and the division of their property. We mediators felt like "pioneers" turning the tides from litigation to mediation for divorcing couples. We didn't realize that we had circled back twenty-five hundred years, at the very least, to recorded times of mediation in which a neutral party between two warring but caring parties helped them to resolve their disputes. In fact, we weren't pioneers in mediation, but we were reaching back to the beginnings of human life on the planet in our application of the process of negotiation to families who were restructuring their households from one into two.

There are many forms of mediation in the world today, most of them with similarities. The Seven Visual Steps to Yes model illustrated in this book is a modified, expanded, visual, and colloquial version of Fisher and Ury's Getting to Yes four-stage model of mediation and the MIT model that began with Howard Raiffa, Larry Susskind, Jeffrey Cruiksank, and many others. It is the model that people can *see* with illustrated cases. I find it most helpful to aid ordinary people—those couples and families with intractable conflicts in their everyday lives—in coming to mutual agreement. I hope you will practice it, use it, and pass it along to those you love and with whom you work.

Acknowledgments

When I first met John Fiske, an attorney with Healy, Fiske, Richmond, and Matthew, in 1980 in Cambridge, Massachusetts, I knew for sure we would work together to form a community of mediation professionals in the Boston area. John, more than I, brought that community together. He, Jerry Weinstein, Joanne Forbes, and I formed the Massachusetts Council on Family Mediation in 1982, which still, thirty-three years later, provides alternate-month professional education in mediation at a very high standard to its members. All mediators in Massachusetts need to acknowledge John's tireless work and attorney David Hoffman's ability to give a stellar presentation on mediator bias to the group. John refers couples to me for decision-making when they are in his office but not ready to create a separation or divorce agreement. He has never completely understood the process by which I help couples make decisions, but this book, dedicated to John, should help to clarify that process—after all these years! My decision making mediation is a prelude to other practitioners's divorce mediation. I do it with couples referred to me for decision making mediation and divorce mediation.

All members of the MCFM continue to contribute to my learning of negotiation and mediation, specifically collaborators of the Negotiation Collaborative: Jeanne Kangas, attorney; Justin Kelsey, attorney; Howard Goldstein, attorney; Chris Chen, CFA, CDFA; and James McCusker, CPA. Susan Miller at Aurora Financial Services is beginning to provide my practice with special family support analyses.

Eliza "Za Za" Jung did research for this book, and Susan Kulton Slyva did an initial copyedit before Timothy Kane did a professional copyedit, and members of Outskirts Press did the final copyedit and reviewed the cover. Without Tim Kane's tireless late-night corrections—taking time away from his wife and two boys—this guide never could have come to fruition. Thank you, Tim. My son, Todd, his wife, Melissa, and two grandchildren, Andrew and Tucker helped me keep writing until this book was done, a very long time, and then told me how "proud" they were upon seeing the cover. Thank you, my family.

For practitioners around the U.S. and around the world desiring to work with groups of pairs who need to make decisions or resolve conflicts by using my power-point slides, the book, and soon a manual, you may contact me at mediationboston@gmail.com. Take a look at www.mediationboston.com for other articles and books written by me.

In the Dominican Republic where I will have a second home in February, 2017, I plan to offer mediated divorces with rapid turn-around times and groups of six to eight pairs who need to make important decisions or resolve conflicts and problems. Come, do the work, walk the 19 miles of white sand beaches, swim, paddle board, surf, kite-board, gallop horses beachside, eat at international restaurants in Las Terrenas. Watch for the development at www.mediationboston.com or call 1-781-861-9847.

Index I

As you begin your negotiation, review the Seven Visual Steps to Yes:
- Step I: Our "I want" positions
- Step II: Our individual basic, bottom-line human needs
- Step III: What *really, really* matters to each of us relative to the conflict
- Step IV: Our individual best personal alternatives
- Step V: Our creative options and ideas
- Step VI: Our supposals and proposals to build agreement
- Step VII: Our mutual agreement

Index II

Skills and Strategies for Decision-Making and Divorce Mediators

1. Make two phone calls, one with each client, for introductions, goal setting, symmetry, and neutrality.
2. Each client states, in the first session, his or her goals for the intervention to attempt to ensure symmetry, neutrality, and equal empowerment.
3. The amount of communication during the session is balanced by the mediator or mediation/decision-making expert who hears from both clients equally.
4. The mediator paraphrases frequently in an attempt to make the partners' statements less toxic and more hearable, understandable, and receivable by the other party.
5. Communication is funneled through the mediator. Clients are not initially permitted to demonstrate their joint repetitive dysfunctional communications or repetition compulsions through fighting in front of the mediator.
6. Blaming, labeling, and accusations are outlawed in this intervention and discouraged at home.
7. "I" statements, not "you are" or "you did" statements, are strongly encouraged.
8. Demonstration of or instruction in the Seven Visual Steps to Yes model is given to all couples.
    a. How to move clients from "I want" positions to what *matters* to each one most (their interests), emphasizing their bottom-line basic needs
    b. How to help clients identify their best personal alternatives and understand why this is important
    c. How to brainstorm *creative* ideas to reach joint solutions

for mutual gains
9. Note: Mutually agreeable solutions are not compromises. Webster's dictionary offers this definition of *compromise*:
   a. a settlement in which each side *gives up* some demands or concessions,
   b. something midway between two other things in quality or effect,
   c. a weakening of one's principles.

I like to think of mutually agreeable solutions as the now familiar "win-win" solutions, *not* as giving up or giving in or weakening one's principles, but as both parties achieving what is most important to him, her, or them.

10. The mediator is "multipartial," not partial to one or the other party; he/she is partial to the best, most creative, and reasonable solution for each of the parties.

Bibliography

1. Burton, John. *Conflict: Human Needs Theory. The Conflict Series. Book* , Palgrave Macmillan,1993.
2. Fisher, Roger, and William Ury., *Getting to Yes.* Random House, 2012.
3. Kelman, Herbert C. *Conflict Resolution and Reconciliation: A Social Psychological Perspective on Ending Violent Conflict between Identity Groups* in *Landscapes of Violence: An Interdisciplinary Journal Devoted to the Study of Violence, Conflict and Trauma.*
4. Maslow, Abraham. *Motivation and Personality, A Theory of Motivation.* 2013
5. Susskind, Lawrence *"Arguing, Bargaining, and Getting Agreement"*, Oxford Handbook of Public Policies. Oxford University Press, New York, 2006.
6. Susskind, Lawrence, and Hallam Movius, *Built to Win: Creating a World Class Negotiation Organization.* Cambridge, MA:

CPSIA information can be obtained
at www.ICGtesting.com
Printed in the USA
LVOW01s0827030916
502878LV00008B/29/P